WINGS IN THE HANDS OF THE LORD

A World War II Journal

LOUIS LaHOOD WITH EVELYN UNES HANSEN
COMPILED BY JIM LaHOOD

Copyrighted Material

Wings in the Hands of the Lord

Copyright © 2018 by James R. LaHood. All Rights Reserved.

No part of this publication may be reproduced, stored in a retrieval system or transmitted, in any form or by any means—electronic, mechanical, photocopying, recording or otherwise—without prior written permission from the publisher, except for the inclusion of brief quotations in a review.

For information about this title or to order other books and/or electronic media, contact the publisher:
James R. LaHood
lahood.jim@gmail.com

ISBN: 978-1-7341599-0-5 (Paperback)
978-1-7341599-1-2 (eBook)

Printed in the United States of America

Cover and Interior design: 1106 Design

Original cover concept by Emily Nieminski

Editorial assistance by Lynne LaHood and Leigh Keylock

Mission illustrations by Barbara LaHood

*With praise and thanks to the Lord,
who rode on my father's wings*

Table of Contents

Foreword		vii
Acknowledgment		xi
1	Elation	1
2	Primary Training	15
3	Basic Training	25
4	Advanced Training	49
5	Transition Training	61
6	Assignment	75
7	Farewell Salute to Home	85
8	East to Debarkation Center	87
9	Destination Ireland	89
10	Night Flight Over the Ocean	95
11	Landfall	101
12	Dismal Christmas	105
13	War — First Glimpse	107

14 Preparing for Missions	109
15 Life at Bassingbourn	111
16 Diary: Bombing Missions	115
Record of Missions	177
17 Homeward Bound	185
18 Closing the Circle	187
19 A Civilian Once Again	193
Epilogue	197

Foreword

In 1977, my father wrote a series of letters to his niece Evelyn, describing his military training and service as a B-17 pilot in World War II. A speech and English professor at the University of Minnesota, Evelyn had prodded him for years to get the story down on paper or to talk about it to serve as a legacy for his family. Sixty-seven double-sided, handwritten pages later, Evelyn had a manuscript to edit and organize into book form, which my father then took to a local bindery. He had enough copies made to hand out to family members and siblings, and surviving crew members (the former of whom had little or no idea of his wartime exploits, other than a few stories from his tenure as a pilot). Everyone knew he had flown 30 successful missions over Germany, but nobody knew any of the details or struggles he had endured, his inner thoughts during and after the war, or honors he had earned.

With these thoughts in mind, it is my desire and that of my three sisters to make our father's compelling story known. It is a story of one ordinary man, yet a struggle experienced by many thousands of young people now called "The Greatest Generation." It is a story about men and women who, if you were to thank them for their service, would reply predictably, "Oh, we were just doing our job."

The first part of this book is the account of Lou LaHood's pilot training, preparing him to lead 30 bombing missions over Germany as a B-17 pilot. The second part contains his thoughts written soon after each mission — describing the target, circumstances, successes, and failures — taken word for word out of his pilot's logbook.

As such, there are statements herein written in the vernacular of the times, not intended to offend any reader, that are simply the words of a young man living through war. In the mission summaries, there are planes mentioned, fellow pilots named, and how they were positioned in the flight pattern. Some official records of the Army Air Forces differ from my father's recollection regarding plane names and positioning on certain missions. However, his summaries were recorded in the present, in the heat of battle. It is important that they are presented as Lou LaHood's honest thoughts at the moment.

This year we celebrate the 75th anniversary of D-Day, the largest invasion ever known to mankind. This year is also the 100th anniversary of my father's birth. If only he were here to celebrate it. Sadly, we lost him to an aggressive brain tumor in 1993. Since his 30th mission occurred a week before D-Day, I believe it is fitting to now share my father's memories with you.

I hope you enjoy them.

Jim LaHood
October 2019

"... that night, the deliberate voice repeated insistently its warning:

'Navigating by the compass in a sea of clouds over Spain is all very well, it is very dashing, but —'

And I was struck by the graphic image:

'But you want to remember that below the sea of clouds lies eternity.'"

Wind, Sand and Stars
by Antoine de Saint Exupery

What follows in these pages is an account of the events that occurred in my life, from the time I entered the United States Armed Forces in 1941, until I was released in 1945. At the request of my niece, I have tried to describe my experiences in writing for our family — past, present, and future.

March 31, 1977
Peoria, Illinois

Acknowledgment

Much of the credit for this book goes to my niece, Evelyn Unes Hansen, who spent many hours, days, and weeks putting all of this information together. She first had to decipher my handwritten manuscript, correct spelling and punctuation, and spend long hours typing, collating, and mimeographing hundreds of pages. But, most of all, I am grateful for the inspiration and encouragement that she has given me.

Evelyn, thank you so very much.

Louis LaHood

CHAPTER 1
Elation

Going through the Air Force Aviation Cadet Training was the greatest period of my life. I just loved every minute of it. The year was 1942. I was accepted after taking a very difficult entrance exam, since I did not have the necessary two years of college that was recommended at that time. The exam consisted of a variety of subjects. There were 150 questions and problems, and a time limit of three and one-half hours to complete. I am very sure that I did not break any records for highest score. In fact, I was positive that I did not come close to passing it. I was astonished when the instructor called two names out of twelve who had taken the exam. Of the twelve, two had passed, and I was one of the two.

I cannot explain the feeling that came over me at that time. It was a feeling of achievement. It gave me more confidence, and it was a feeling of tremendous joy, because

I had a strong desire to fly airplanes at that time. I wanted to get into the Air Force so badly that I think I would have been crushed if I had failed that exam.

I think it would not have been so difficult had they allowed us to study for it, read a couple of textbooks, or something, but if I remember correctly, there wasn't time for any of that. A notice was posted on the bulletin board one day that the exam for the Air Force was going to be offered in a few days, so we had to sign up right then.

I was given my orders to pack my belongings and go home, until such time I would receive orders to report for Air Cadet training. My Army buddies were very envious of me, and I was glad to get out of the walking Army. I had been drafted into the regular Army from Peoria, Illinois, on April 2, 1941, and had just spent the most miserable year of my life in Army service. Basic training was the worst. Marching and drilling in the hot North Carolina sun, picking up papers and cigarette butts on the grounds every day, KP a week or two at a time. Obstacle courses until I was sore all over. Bivouacs in the Louisiana swamps, sleeping out on the ground, in the rain and mud, taking a bath in an old stagnant water hole, scared to death of snakes — and there were plenty of them. As I said, I was glad to leave all of that, so I didn't waste any time getting out of there.

At the time, I was stationed at Camp Roberts, California, from which I was to return to Peoria to wait for my orders from the Air Force. I had no problem deciding the means of transportation back to Peoria, as the United States Army in 1941 was not noted for being the highest-paying service company in the world. I believe I had just received a promotion and was earning a salary of $30 per month — a lot better than the $21 a month I had been earning prior to the promotion. At my salary, I did not have the money to take a train or a plane or even a bus, so the next best thing was the thumb!

It was May, the weather was nice, and I had a lot of time. I thought I might as well hitchhike home and see the country. I had to go through Sacramento, and because I wanted to visit my Uncle Johnny and Aunt Kathryn, who, at that time, were living in a town called Vallejo, I hitched a ride up there and stayed with them for a few days. I hadn't seen them for several years, so we had a lot to talk about. They had no idea that I was coming, so they were quite surprised to see me. I stayed a couple of days, and we had a very enjoyable visit.

Aunt Kathryn couldn't believe that I was going to hitchhike all the way back to Peoria. She pleaded with me not to, giving all sorts of reasons why I shouldn't try it:

"It's too far. You never know what kinds of people you'll meet on the road. It gets awfully cold at night in the mountains. What if you are on the road at night — where will you sleep?"

They even offered me money to take a train, but I refused because I wanted to go through with my plans. I was 22 years old, eager for a little adventure, and not at all worried about the trip.

So I said, "No, just take me out to the highway, and I will start thumbing."

Well, they drove me all the way to Sacramento. It was a nice drive, and we stopped along the way to see some interesting sights. When we reached the highway where I was going to start thumbing, Aunt Kathryn insisted they stay with me until I got a ride, and in spite of my assurances that that wasn't necessary, they stayed anyway. Before long, a car came down the road; the driver saw me and stopped to pick me up. She was a rather elderly lady, alone, and she asked if I would like to ride with her. As I was getting into the car, Aunt Kathryn came running over to the car, pointed her finger at the lady, and said,

"You take good care of this boy."

As it turned out, the ride was not very long, as she was just going about five miles down the road. Had I bothered to ask how far she was going, I may not have accepted the ride.

After she let me out, I caught another ride with a nice family, who took me quite a distance. Going from Sacramento to Reno, Nevada, there is a summit to cross where, even in summer, there is almost always snow. When we reached the summit, the road was covered by two feet of snow, and many cars were stuck or stalled. Seeing that, the people I was riding with decided to turn back rather than risk going farther, but I decided to try to get through with someone else. I thanked them, got out, and started walking up a hill where, at the top, I saw a lodge which was used by skiers on skiing vacations. I went in, but, of course, no rooms were available because they had all been rented by all the people stranded by the snow. I can remember seeing people sleeping all over the floor in the lobby. The dining room, where I had a sandwich and a cup of coffee, was doing a land-office business, and lines to the restrooms were 20 yards long at all times. I read every magazine in the building and then finally curled up on the floor and went to sleep.

By morning, the snow had stopped, the weather was turning a little warmer, and cars were beginning to move out again. Once again, I set out along the highway, and, soon, a car with three young ladies between the ages of 25 and 30 years stopped. They said they were afraid to go down the mountain alone and asked if I would like to ride with them. I accepted, but before we moved on, I helped put snow chains on their tires, and then we started out, with two of the women sitting in the front seat and the third lying in the back. I couldn't help but notice, although I tried not to seem impolite by looking at her, that the girl in back was in a body cast from the waist down. They explained that she was their sister, that she had been in a bad accident in California, and now, after a long hospitalization there, they were taking her home to Reno. We drove for hours, slipping and sliding a little, and stopping now and then so that I could readjust the tire chains. Finally, we got to Reno.

I asked to be let out on the highway so I could catch another ride, but they asked me if I could please come to their house to help carry their sister in, as there was no one else there. I said I would. After we pulled up to their house, I had one heck of a time trying to get her out of that car. It was a two-door, and the front seat didn't go down and forward far enough, but we finally got her out without any further injury, and I carried her into the house and put her on the sofa. They couldn't thank me enough. By this time, it was getting late in the evening, and they were worried about me hitching a ride at night. I said it would be all right, but they insisted that I stay in town overnight, and they gave me $10.00 to go and get a hotel room; so I did just that. But before I turned in for the night, I browsed around town for a while, went to a couple of bars, and saw practically all the casinos. Reno was really a live town at that time — a lot of soldiers roaming around and lots of gaiety.

I don't know why it was, but it seemed that the bars in every town in the country during World War II did a

*Fort Bragg, North Carolina
1941*

flourishing business. Husbands were gone to service, and wives were out having a good time. Everyone lived as if there were no tomorrow. I will never forget when I was in basic training in Fort Bragg, North Carolina, the town was full of soldiers, and it was so obvious that practically every girl you would see walking down the street was pregnant. We used to bet each other a beer to see who could count the most pregnant girls.

After spending the night in Reno, I left the next morning, heading for Salt Lake City. I got a ride with five tough-looking guys in a great big black sedan who looked to me like a bunch of gangsters. After hearing some of their conversation in the car as we drove along, I was beginning to be convinced that they were. They had a bottle of booze, and they were passing it around and driving really fast and crazily. I was scared to death. They had me sitting in the back seat between two thugs, and I didn't dare open my mouth. Every once in a while, they would offer me a drink, which I would refuse. Then they would laugh and say,

"What'sa matter, soldier — don't you drink?"

I didn't think I was going to get out of that car alive. I could just see us going off of one of those cliffs at any minute. As we were going over the mountain, snow began falling again, and the further we drove, the more snow there was on the ground. We drove for about six hours and, by then, I was a nervous wreck. I was almost ready to ask for some of that booze, but I was too afraid to talk.

My heart was in my mouth as we headed up a steep incline, the car skidding along and sliding toward the side of the road, and then finally hitting a snow bank and coming to a sudden stop. The car was half buried by the snow, but I said to myself, "Thank God! At least we're not moving any more," and that was all I was concerned about. We all piled out, and the brains of the outfit sized up the situation and started giving orders to all of the other guys. It was a riot. At his orders, we all started pushing while he drove. The more we pushed, the more he spun the wheels; the more he spun the wheels, the deeper the car lodged itself in the snow. All the time we were pushing, I was praying that the car would get so deep it would never get out. No way did I want to get back in and ride with those guys again.

My prayers were answered when, after about an hour of our shoving and digging and their cussing and yelling, a car came up the road, the driver saw us in trouble, and he stopped; although there was nothing he could do, he asked if he could be of some help.

"Shall I send a tow truck back from the next town?" he asked the "head honcho," who answered, "Yeah."

When the driver saw the insignia on my uniform, he called me over and told me that he was a retired general of the Army; he said that he used to be in command of the division that I was in and asked me what I was doing with this bunch. I told him that I had hitched a ride with them.

He said, "Get in my car." Without even bothering to say "Thanks," I grabbed my duffle bag, jumped into his car, and away we went. I was so relieved to get away from that bunch of clowns.

Believe it or not, I rode with him for almost two whole days. He was a very nice guy; he treated me like a long-lost son, he bought my meals, and we talked for hours. I was a good listener, and he liked that; he told me his life story of his Army career. We stayed overnight in Salt Lake City at a swanky hotel, where he got me a separate room and where we ate dinner that evening in their beautiful dining room. He was retired, had a lot of money, and had never had any children of his own. He took me all the way to Denver, where I believe he lived, as he said it was as far as he was going. I found him very interesting to listen to, and I really enjoyed his company. He was interested in my future in the Air Force; he gave me his name and address, and told me to write and tell him how I was doing. But I think I got too involved and too busy, and I never did write him. I always felt guilty about that. I thanked him very much for everything, and we parted.

From Denver, I had several different rides. By this time, I guess I had spent about six days on the road. I finally got to St. Louis and was very tired and eager to get home. Now within range where I could afford to buy a bus ticket, I took a bus from St. Louis to Peoria. How much it cost I don't remember, but I don't suppose it was more than two dollars. Hitchhiking from California, although a little rough at times, was a tremendous experience. It is one week I will never forget.

While waiting for orders to arrive in Peoria, I think I lived with my brother George and Mary, his wife. In all, I stayed in Peoria for about 60 days, and people were beginning to think that I was AWOL. In fact, it was getting to be embarrassing. But finally, I received my orders to report. Where else? Santa Ana, California. So, back I went, except this time by train at their expense.

I hung around Santa Ana Air Base for about 30 days before being assigned to a regular Pre-Flight Training School. While waiting around with nothing to do, we would go into Los Angeles and Hollywood. We took tours through movie studios, watched them shoot a few movies, and met a lot of nice people. Then, in August of 1942, I received my orders to report to Maxwell Field in Montgomery, Alabama, to begin Cadet Training.

Aviation Cadet Training consisted of four phases of instruction: 1. Pre-Flight, 2. Primary, 3. Basic, 4. Advanced — approximately 12 weeks in each.

> Pre-Flight consisted of nothing but ground school and very rigid discipline. Classroom subjects were mathematics, physics, navigation, military customs, communications, cryptography, meteorology, aircraft identification, aerodynamics, aircraft construction and mechanical operation, and more. You do not see an airplane in Pre-Flight School.

Primary is the first actual flying you get to do. It is the most fun. The planes are two-wing, open-cockpit planes, similar to those used in World War I.

Basic is a step up into a little more powerful plane — a two-seater with closed canopy and about a 450-horsepower engine.

Advanced is just what the word implies. The plane is somewhat larger and has a 600-horsepower engine and a lot more sophisticated instruments — more equipment, more detailed flying, more specialized.

Pre-Flight

Pre-Flight was very tough, not only from an academic standpoint but also from the intensive drilling, discipline, and most of all, the hazing from upperclassmen and the physical conditioning. We had classroom study for five hours a day. Three days a week, after classes, we had physical conditioning. Two days a week, we ran a six-mile trail they called the "Indian Trail," keeping perfect formation. The trail was all on flat ground, and we ran it after an hour of calisthenics. But I enjoyed the running; we were getting in good shape.

Another trail was called the "Burma Road," and we ran that once or sometimes twice a week. It was about five miles long and involved running up hills, through water holes, over obstacles, trees, ditches, fences, swinging on ropes, scaling a hill that had 75 or 100 steps cut into the ground, and when you ran up those steps, your legs were so tired you could hardly lift them. It was a killer. As a matter of fact, one guy had a heart attack and died while running it. Alabama was still extremely hot in September, and you really sweat and drink water by the gallon. After running the Burma Road in that heat, you didn't need anyone to rock you to sleep at night!

Pre-Flight School was, in fact, a poor man's West Point. However, I believe the 10 weeks of discipline and military training is as intense as that at West Point or the Air Force Academy. Our living quarters were long buildings, with all the rooms, about 20 in each, lined up side by side on one floor, as in a motel. Each room opened onto a screened-in porch or stoop, which ran the entire length of the building. All the buildings were set around the perimeter of, with all rooms facing, the athletic field or parade grounds, where our drilling, parades, and athletic events took place. So, you could look out your window and see what was going on out there at any time. There were two guys to a room.

Ground school was very tough, and there was a lot of studying at night in the room. You had to try to study and also beware of upperclassmen, who would take a notion to barge into your room at any time to inspect it for neatness, or just do anything they wanted to, to harass you. If they decided that things were not to their satisfaction, they would give you a certain number of laps to run or walk around the parade grounds. These were to be done either at night or on Sunday, during your free time. Going to the dining room for meals was done in formation after the whole group assembled. And it had to be marched in perfect formation, with everyone dressed perfectly — clothes clean and pressed, no wrinkles in the pants or shirt, shoes shined, neckties and hats, and no buttons open or missing or, buddy, you were in trouble. You would march and sing the Air Force song, "Off we go, into the wild blue yonder," and you had better sound off. You would stand at attention for what seemed like an hour while they inspected you, all the while yelling,

"Come on, mister, shoulders back! Suck in that gut! Get that chin in! Get the wrinkles out of that shirt!"

And when you finally arrived at the mess hall, you had better remain standing until the upperclassmen were seated and told you to sit down. When you sat down to eat, you would not look at anything except your plate in front of you. You sat straight up, staring at your plate. An upperclassman sat near you, and you did not say,

"Please pass the meat." You said,

"Sir, Mr. LaHood would like some meat, please. Sir, Mr. LaHood would like some bread, please."

You sat there and waited until he was ready to pass it to you. When you did finally get your food, you had to eat a "square meal" — that is, lift your fork straight up from your plate, move it at a right angle to your mouth and back out straight, and then down to your plate again. This went on every day, and besides being almost unbearable, it also made you want to commit murder.

Our screened porches on the buildings were about 12 feet wide, and an underclassman was never allowed to walk down the center. You walked along either side and made darned sure you touched your shirt to the wall. A fire extinguisher hung on the wall, and every time you walked by it, you saluted that fire extinguisher, or you were in bad trouble. Nor could you walk at a slow pace, either. When you walked on that porch, you were almost in a trot! One day, an upperclassman pulled up my pant legs to see if my

*Louis LaHood
U.S. Army, 1941*

socks were hanging down. Of course, they were. So, he made me stand on the busiest corner of the base, with my pants rolled up to my knees, and tell everyone who walked by,

"I was a bad boy today, 'cause I did not wear my garters."

The only consolation was in knowing that someday, when we became upperclassmen, we would be able to put underclassmen through the same paces.

Miraculously, I survived Pre-Flight School without washing out. I think it was only because I had such a burning desire to succeed. Before going into the Air Force, I had read a book, the title of which, regrettably, I have since forgotten. The book was about how to attain all of your personal goals through a positive mental attitude. It was a super-good book! I read it a lot; I began to adopt this way of life, and I have always since lived by it. I soon developed a strong faith and self-confidence, knowing that there was a good chance to succeed at anything, if you maintained a positive mental attitude.

Pre-Flight — the hard work, tough discipline, physical conditioning, long and boring classwork — was a drag. What a beautiful feeling it was when we had finished, and the day finally came when we could throw off the anxiety we had felt and enjoy the anticipation of going on to the next phase, which was actually learning to fly.

CHAPTER 2

Primary Training

I could hardly wait to see where I would be sent, hoping for Florida, as, by then, it was November, and I wanted to go somewhere warm. Sure enough, I was assigned to Carlstrom Field in Arcadia, Florida, a small town in the center of the state.

I don't remember how we traveled from Alabama to Florida, but I think it was by train. It seemed like forever before we got there, and I was so eager to see the planes and the field and our living quarters. You can believe this or not, but previous to this moment, I had never been on an airplane, or for that matter, even near one! I mean near enough to see it closely. Of course, I had seen them in the air, but never at hands-on distance. Where or how I developed such a strong fascination, I don't know, but I had a tremendous desire to fly, and it so overwhelmed me at that time that I just couldn't wait to get my hands on a plane.

16 ✈ WINGS IN THE HANDS OF THE LORD

Upon arrival at Arcadia, Florida, we were transported by bus from the train depot to the airfield. More like a country club than a military installation, the field was beautiful and just as I had pictured it! The living quarters were built of brick, the rooms were neat and clean, and there were swimming pools, tennis courts, a golf course, and a recreation hall where dances were held every couple of weeks. I was thrilled to be there, and I couldn't wait to start flying instructions. On our first day there, we received our room assignments. Although there were four men to a room, we were not crowded, for the rooms were pleasant and spacious enough for two double bunk beds, a couple of lounge chairs, a table, and one bath. I was in with three super-great guys, all Irishmen: Fogarty, Farley, Finnegan, and LaHood. How do you like that for a

Fogarty, Farley, LaHood
Arcadia, Florida
December 1942

foursome? How in the world I ever got put in with them, I'll never know, but as long as I live, I'll never regret it, for we came to be the best of friends — more like brothers, in fact. Although we roomed together for only about 12 weeks, we developed a deep friendship which, even after all these years, we still have. In struggling together for the same goal, we formed a bond among ourselves that has never been broken. We lied for each other, we covered for each other, we worried about each other when we were flying, we played sports together, we went on dates together; there was just nothing we wouldn't do for each other.

Fogarty was a super piano player, and every night when we gathered in the recreation hall, he played the piano while we all sang. He played in a band in civilian life, and

Lou hoisted by unidentified classmate while Fogarty, Farley, and Finnegan look on Arcadia, Florida December 1942

he was so good! He was also a super good-looking guy. He lived in Akron, Ohio.

Merle Farley was the happy-go-lucky playboy. Good looking also, he was a late-night guy who was always trying to find a nice girl. Unfortunately, there were not many good ones around an Air Force base. Merle was a late sleeper, and we would have to shake the sheets to get him up in the morning. He now lives in Davenport, Iowa, and comes to Peoria occasionally to visit me.

Billy Finnegan, a clean-cut guy and very smart, was the studious one. We called him "the preacher." He was very articulate and a perfectionist — neat and clean in appearance and a very good athlete. He never ran around with girls or took a drink of alcohol; he always had a smile on his face. Although we had known each other in Pre-Flight, we hadn't lived close to each other. But here, sharing the same room for 12 weeks, I think we were as close as any four guys could get to be.

On our second day at Arcadia, we were to report to the flight line to meet our flying instructor. Just to get that close to the airplanes had to be my biggest thrill to that point. When we got down there that second morning, it was so fascinating to see all the planes lined up in front of the hangars, some with motors running, some taxiing, ready for takeoff; the smell of gasoline and the sound of tires squealing added to the excitement. It was the beginning of a new and thrilling time in my life, and I had butterflies in my stomach. Joe Carlon, the instructor I was assigned to, was from Galesburg, Illinois. When he found out that I was from Peoria, we got to be pretty good friends, until, of course, I started to make a lot of mistakes; then I was just another dumb cadet to him.

Every instructor had five students and spent one hour a day with each of them. We spent five hours a day on the flight line and four hours in ground school — 7:00 a.m. to 12:00 noon flying, and 1:00 p.m. to 5:00 p.m. in school. The first time we went up, the instructor just took us for a ride, and he did all the flying.

The training planes were two-wing, single-engine Stearman PT-17s, two-seaters with open cockpits — very stable, capable of any kind of maneuver, and really fun to fly. After our familiarization ride, we each had a half hour of instructions. When he called my name for my first half-hour instruction ride, I was shaking all over.

"Who, me?" I asked.

I didn't know whether to faint or turn around and run, or say "I quit," or what to do. Instinctively, I guess, I just walked out to the plane in a daze. We took off, and I think

Lou climbing aboard Stearman PT-17 training plane
Arcadia, Florida
December 1942

my stomach stayed on the ground. I could feel myself getting sick and weak, and I asked myself, "What the heck am I doing here?" The instructor, meanwhile, was making steep turns and some other maneuvers, all the while explaining them on the intercom. He demonstrated a stall and a roll and a steep climb, and by that point, my stomach was all upset. I was dizzy, and right then, I was convinced that I could never do this. I was ready to resign.

Then he said, "You take the controls now, and fly straight and even for a while."

I did, and it was OK.

Then, after a while, he said, "Now make a turn, and then another and another."

Before long, I began to feel in control of the plane. I did a few more things that added to my confidence, and after about a half hour, I began to like it more. The next day, the actual lessons began: fundamentals, procedures, landings, and takeoffs for hours, and then stalls, spins, rolls, and all kinds of aerobatics. I was beginning to like it more and more. We received only eight hours of instruction with an instructor before we had to solo. To prepare us, he taught us how to do lazy eights and pylon eights, which are nothing more than figure eights flown perfectly. To achieve that perfection, you pick a stationary object on the ground, and, using that as a focal point, you fly so that your wing tip maintains the same distance going around it and hold the plane so that it neither gains nor loses any altitude at all. In addition, he instructed us how to do a stall. A stall is just what it says — a stall. You climb at a steep angle, until the plane will not climb any higher. Like a car going up a steep hill, without feeding it gas, the car will eventually come to a stop. The same with a plane. Climb at a steep angle with a fixed throttle, and the plane will eventually stall, and when it does, it goes completely out of control and starts to fall.

It's essential to know how to get a plane under control again under such conditions, and that's why they teach the stall. It's quite a simple principle, really: if you have enough altitude, you simply push the nose of the plane down and get some more air speed, and then you are flying again. The reason planes crash is that, when they stall out at a low altitude, they don't have enough altitude to get flying speed again, and that's when they hit the ground. If a plane stalls on takeoff, you've had it, unless there is a field straight ahead to set it down. A plane will also go into a spin after a stall if it falls to one side or the other.

After about the third or fourth time up, we learned how to do spins. To spin a plane, you climb very high, so that you have a safe amount of altitude in case you have trouble getting it out. When you have about 8,000 feet, you head it straight up so it will stall, and then you step on the left or right rudder, depending on which way you want to spin. The plane falls out of control to the side you hit the rudder, and then you begin to spin downward. When you think you have spun enough and you want to return to normal, you hit the opposite rudder from the direction you are spinning and, at the same time, pull back on the stick, and you should come out of it and return to straight and level. You hope! At times, planes do not react immediately, and that's when you start sweating.

You're trying to do all these things with your instructor barking at you constantly. My theory on learning military flying is that they want to keep men under extreme pressure while learning, because combat flying is constant pressure under extremely adverse conditions. They reason, consequently, that if you are good enough to hack it in training under all this pressure, you might qualify as a combat pilot. It's definitely unlike learning in civilian life, where you pay an instructor $20 for a lesson, and he talks nice to you, is very polite, and has a lot of patience. I would hesitate to use the language in this book that was used on us in the Air Force. You can get the picture by imagining being screamed at constantly, called all kinds of dumb names, and being the object of profanities that are "something else."

Their most famous phrase was, "All right, dummy, get your head out of your ass!"

And when they got good and mad and impatient, they'd take the controls and fly you upside down for a while or put you in a spin and scare the crap out of you.

This primary flying was the most fun, though, and I began to love it. After our eight hours of dual instruction, we were ready to solo. Wow! That was an exciting day. The first time I soloed, I got up in the air and was flying around and just having a wonderful time. I was doing all the maneuvers that I had learned with my instructor, when all of a sudden, I pushed the throttle all the way forward to do a climb or something, and the darned throttle stuck forward, and I couldn't get it back. The motor was racing as fast as it could. Of course, I immediately panicked! At the time, I was only about two miles away from the main field. I remember being so frightened that I blacked out momentarily. The first thing I could think of to do was to pull the ripcord on my parachute, and, in my panic, I almost did exactly that while still sitting in the cockpit. Fortunately, in a few seconds, I came to my senses and decided to look for an auxiliary field to land at. Luckily, there was a practice field right below me, so I killed the engine, went down, and made a forced landing. It was very simple; we had practiced forced landings a lot.

When I got down, I felt very proud of myself. I thought, *Boy, my instructor is going to be really proud of me for making a soft landing, and all that.* So I sent word back to the main field for them to come and get me. And soon, here came my instructor. Someone had driven him over in a truck. I was all ready for some praise, when, all of a sudden, he lit into me with some of the best cuss words you have ever heard.

He said, "You stupid ass! What did you land here for? You were only two miles from the field. So what if the damn throttle was stuck, you dummy? You could have brought it back there as well as here. All you had to do was shut the son of a bitch off and glide the rest of the way. But it figures. You haven't got enough brains to do that. All right, dummy! Get in, and I'll take you back to the field, with a stuck throttle."

Boy, did we get a fast ride back! He never let me forget it, either.

From then on, I learned a lot about flying. When you are up there alone, you learn more than you do with an instructor. We had to go up every day and do all the aerobatics and all the maneuvers we had learned, and then we had to take little cross-country trips. Plot a course on a map, go for two or three hours, and get back on time. All of these things we had to do to perfection, and, at the end of the course, we were checked and graded by someone other than our own instructor.

The check pilot was tough. Either you did it right, or you were out. The washout rate was 50–60%. I was very nervous on my check ride, but, fortunately, I passed. All of us in our room — Farley, Finnegan, Fogarty, and LaHood — passed, and we went out and celebrated that night.

Even after all the primary instructions were finished, we stayed there for a few more weeks, flying every day on practice maneuvers and cross-country trips — just far enough away to get some flying time and practice. I loved flying there. I loved the airplane. It was so stable and maneuverable that, no matter what you did with it, it would come back to normal practically by itself. For example, if you spin this plane, it comes out of the spin by itself, just by your letting go of the controls, whereas a more powerful plane has to be brought out of a spin by fighting the controls. Hard to believe, but we had spent almost 12 weeks at this base, and we had had so much fun. When we were not flying or in school, we would either be playing ball or swimming or playing golf. It had been great, and we hated to leave when, soon thereafter, we got our orders to report to another base for further training.

CHAPTER 3

Basic Training

For our next phase, basic training, we were sent to a place called Bainbridge, Georgia, the worst hellhole of all, I think, in the whole United States. Coming from a country club in Florida, maybe we were spoiled, but honestly, this place was depressing. Where we had been used to nice living quarters, pleasant warm weather, and green trees and swimming pools, here we had nothing but bare ground and no grass, but lots of dust and dirt and cold weather. By now, if I remember correctly, it was December or January. Our living quarters — just regular Army barracks with no individual rooms and 20 guys to a building — were terrible; there were just a bunch of bunks as the only furnishings. To add to the unpleasantness, our foursome of Fogarty, Farley, Finnegan, and LaHood was split up and not even assigned to the same building. We tried to keep in contact, but from here on, things became hectic, and we were not able to be together often.

Our basic trainer, the BT-13, was a larger plane — a single-wing, single-engine with a 450-horsepower motor. It had a closed cockpit with a sliding glass canopy. Insofar as it was noisier than what we were used to, it was a scary plane. For flight instructors, we had a bunch of cocky guys who had graduated from this same training, maybe two or three years ahead of us, and stayed on as instructors. Bill Martin, my instructor, was a young guy of 25 or 26 from Philadelphia, Pennsylvania. Just a really cocky guy who thought he knew everything, full of wise remarks but never a straight answer about anything. You had to be extra perfect with him; he was the kind of guy who would wash you out just because he didn't like your looks. We didn't get along well. I didn't like him, and I am sure he didn't like me. Another instructor, who was one of his good buddies, was even worse than Martin; between the two of them, they washed out more guys than all of the other instructors combined. Fortunately, Captain Williams, our commanding officer, was an understanding and good man.

The irony of this is that these men got to be instructors because they did not want to go to combat. They were always scared to death that someday they would have to go overseas. You see, this was just after Pearl Harbor, where we had suffered such heavy losses. We were trying to build up our Air Force in a hurry, and the Air Force was badly in need of flying instructors. So, men who graduated two or three classes ahead of us were given the option of staying to instruct or going to combat. Naturally, a lot of them chose to stay. Unfortunately, they were the worst kind — the kind who thought they were something special because they wore a pair of silver wings.

Because this phase of training involved more instrument flying and more navigational aids, it was rougher. We now had radio communication, something we did not have in the primary trainer. Our ground school, too, was getting more complicated, with rigorous studies in navigation and meteorology. We began, for the first time, to do a lot of night flying. Night flying was particularly hard for me, because I did not have good night vision, a characteristic, I believe, of our family. Had the Air Force known this about me, they would have washed me out immediately; so, of course, I did all I could to conceal that knowledge from them. I always passed the eye tests OK, and I never mentioned my condition to the flight surgeon for fear I'd be gone. So, I struggled along. As long as the runway lights were on, it was a snap for me, and I was all right.

Our instructions in the BT-13 began right away, and, for the first week or so, things were basically the same as what we had learned before in primary training. We were more or less just getting used to the larger plane, doing stalls, spins, rolls, loops, takeoffs, and landings. Gradually, we began plotting out longer cross-country trips, flying the radio beam from one town to another, taking night cross-country trips using several different navigational aids such as beacons, beams, and light lines. Light lines are a series of red lights placed about 20 miles apart in a line from one town to another.

Then, in addition to our flying and ground school, we began to learn instrument flying in a link trainer, a small airplane similar to a toy airplane on a platform that a child might ride for a quarter at a supermarket. Except this very scientific machine was no toy. Housed inside buildings, the trainers were completely closed so that you could not see out at all and had to depend entirely on instruments. The purpose was to fly a complete course on instruments. The controls in the trainer were just like those in a plane, and using those controls, you simulated an actual flight by flying a predetermined course, all of which was recorded on paper. You would take up certain compass headings for a certain number of minutes, and then, depending on how many miles your destination was and your airspeed, you would change course for a certain length of time. You had to calculate how long to fly a certain heading to reach your destination at a certain speed, and when you thought you had reached the field of your destination, you would call for landing instructions and make an instrument landing. Sometimes you would miss the field by two miles if you hadn't flown your flight accurately. There was a required number of hours of link trainer, and we were graded on how well we did. It was hard, and it was very warm inside the trainer, with each simulated flight lasting about an hour. But, in spite of all, it was interesting. And, although some guys just hated it, I always enjoyed it and found it to be a good way to learn instrument flying.

Soloing in a BT-13 required more dual instructions than soloing in a PT-17 — I think about 10 days of one hour a day of dual flying. The first time I soloed a BT-13, I was scared to death! It was a monster! Big, noisy, and hard to handle. And when you got it rolling down the runway, getting up enough speed to take off, it would shake and shimmy, and you thought surely it was going to fall apart. When you came in for a landing, it acted the same way, except then, it seemed as if the wheels were going to fall off. And after the way the students bounced those planes in, it's a wonder the wheels didn't fall off. On your first few landings, I'm sure you bounce at least 10 feet in the air. In fact, every landing is pretty rough, and those landing gears take a terrible beating.

Visibility in this plane was not the greatest, either. The glass canopies had some distortion, and sun shining on the canopies caused a glare. At night, too, visibility was strange as the cockpit lights reflected on the glass, causing confusion and sometimes causing the illusion that the lights were from something on the ground, and then you would panic and think you were flying upside down. There were a lot of fears and frustrations at times. But, nevertheless, it was still a lot of fun.

As I said earlier, we began doing a lot of night flying, takeoffs, landings, and night cross-country via radio beams. Then came the cruncher. We were going to start practicing blackout landings! Wow! I was scared to death. Up until now, it hadn't been bad because we used runway lights and wing lights. But now we were going over to some auxiliary field with no lights and shoot blackout takeoffs and landings. Having told us that, they said, however, that we would not begin these exercises for about a week or two. From then on, naturally, everyone was uptight. Had it not been for the instructors we had — a bunch of bastards — this phase of training would not have been so bad. I had the urge, at least a hundred times, to kill mine. But as bad as mine was, he had a buddy, Don Franks, who was the worst one of the bunch — a little guy with a loud voice. I think he had a complex because of his size; yelling and cussing and pulling his rank on you was a way to inflate his ego. Whenever any instructor wanted to give his student a bad time, he would ask Don Franks to ride with him. In our class, we had a big kid, about 6'2" and 195 pounds, who was a really nice guy. He was part Indian, and, as a former football player at Texas A&M, he was rough and tough. Whenever we'd have a game of touch football, he would just about put all of us in the hospital. We called him Bigfoot.

Bigfoot was a big, good-looking guy, easygoing until someone rubbed him the wrong way. Then he had a violent temper. Well, anyway, I guess he was having trouble with his instructor; so, they arranged for him to ride with Don Franks. Next day, they went up together and, as expected, Franks started chewing on him. Franks put him through every maneuver he could think of, and, according to Don, Bigfoot did not do anything right. I imagine Franks screamed and cussed at him the whole time. Finally, they were shooting some running takeoffs and landings, where you come in and land the plane, but instead of rolling to a stop, halfway down the runway, you give it the gun and take off again. They had done several, by which time Bigfoot was so fed up with all the name calling, he just landed the plane and let it roll to a stop. He taxied over to the ramp, shut off the engine, climbed out of his cockpit and onto the wing, opened up Franks' canopy, grabbed him by the parachute straps, and pulled him right out of his seat, onto the wing, and down to the ground. With fire in his eyes, he looked straight at Franks and said,

"All right, you little son of a bitch, now call me those names again."

Franks turned white as a sheet and kept silent, probably at this point fearing for his life. Whereupon Bigfoot grabbed him again by his jacket and lifted him up and down a couple of times and slammed him down to the ground. Franks was petrified! He scrambled to his feet and dashed into the flight room. After he calmed down a bit, he went in and reported the incident to Captain Williams. The next day, Bigfoot was called into Williams' office. Captain Williams was a very understanding, calm, and easygoing guy, and always discussed things in a calm and quiet manner. He simply asked Bigfoot exactly what had happened up there.

So Bigfoot told him, "From the very moment we took off, he started yelling and screaming about everything I did. Nothing I did was right, and never once did he correct me or tell me how to do it properly. He just cussed at me the whole time. After about a half hour of that, I figured I'd had enough, and especially so after he had called me a 'dumb Indian.' Nobody calls me that and lives to tell it, even if he is an officer."

Captain Williams listened intently to his testimony and said, "Well, you can return to your quarters. I will not punish you this time, but see that a thing like this never happens again."

I am sure that Williams was fully aware of Franks' tactics. Although I don't know for sure, I suspect that Mr. Franks heard something from Captain Williams, too, for, after that incident, Franks was not as loud and arrogant as he had been.

After several days of night cross-country trips and night takeoffs and landings on the main field with lighted runways, we were finally ready to begin our blackout landings. Up to this time, I was doing quite well, flying at night from the main field, taking solo trips, shooting solo landings; my skill was improving. I had never gotten lost on a trip; I was learning how to fly the radio beam well enough to get from one town to another. However, I was beginning to fear the day when we'd start blackout landings. The auxiliary field where they taught blackout landings was nothing but a grassy field. It had no concrete runways. You can imagine what worried me: my night vision, already less than perfect, would be all the worse without a little light, at least, reflected off a concrete runway. Especially if the moon was shining, a concrete runway gave off enough light to help me see a little better.

At the auxiliary field, there was neither tower nor radio as at our regular field. Instead, they had a portable system in a truck or a van, and we established communication with operators in the vehicle who sometimes had to talk us down on the radio. If we were coming in too high or too low, they told us to correct; if we couldn't make it at all, they would shout, "Take it up and go around again!"

Our first experience at the auxiliary field came at about half, or maybe two-thirds of the way, through basic training, when we had gotten well used to flying this plane we had been learning. I had prayed — oh, how I had prayed — for a full moon. But naturally, they had chosen a dark night; there was no full moon. The only light came from two small dark blue lights at the end of the runway — the path we were to use for landing — and those lights denoted the end of the field. The lights were so dim they were hardly visible at all, but yet, they were something. On our first night, there were probably six planes there, and we would take off one after another and get in the traffic pattern, waiting for our separate clearances from the radio truck to peel off and come in to land. Of course, we were all with instructors. There would be no soloing for quite a while yet.

We all took off and got into the pattern, and, of course, we had to be at a safe distance because it was so dark. After we had flown around a couple of times, the first plane got clearance to land, and the instructor, demonstrating the technique, brought it down. Each instructor followed down in turn. Next it was the students' turn to try. The first guy peeled off and came in. And from there on, the conversation on the radio waves would have made a terrific old-time Laurel and Hardy movie. Everybody was shouting orders and directions and screaming and cussing.

"Pull up! Go to left, dummy; you're off the runway! Not so high, slow down, hold it there — I said hold it there, you screwball; you want to kill us? Oh, hell, go around — we'll never make it!"

"OK, LaHood — your turn."

I peeled off, and my instructor screamed, "Don't turn the SOB on its back! What the hell are you doing?!!"

I saw the reflection of the cockpit lights on the canopy and thought I was upside down. I whipped it over and there I was, heading straight down at the ground, going about 195 mph, when he grabbed the stick and straightened us out.

"OK, you dumb shit. Let's go around and try it again. This time, don't stand it on its wing."

We went around again, and I peeled off a little less this time and got in line with the runway, but I wasn't descending fast enough.

"Down! Get her down! How in the hell are you going to land it way up here?" Going 100 mph, I couldn't see how far I was off the ground. Shucks, I was lucky to find the blue lights.

"Give her the gun! We'll go around. Hell, you haven't got enough field to land now, anyway."

Around we went again, peeled off, got in line with the blue lights and runway, and he started talking me down:

"OK, down! Down! Let off the throttle; how the hell are you going to get down?"

Frightened, I yanked back the throttle, and boy, did we come down — bang! We hit the ground, bounced about 15 feet, and then, bang! We hit the ground again and again before finally rolling smooth. Then he gave it the throttle and took off again.

He said, "Boy, we are going to try this a couple more times tonight, and then we are going to quit. You are making a nervous wreck out of me."

After flying around a few more times, nothing had changed; I was all over the place — bouncing, running off the runway, climbing too fast, diving too steep, turning too sharp.

He was disgusted: "OK, let's quit for now. An hour and a half of that is enough for one night."

Not much consolation, but I wasn't the only one who had done poorly; not one guy in the bunch had any decent landings.

"OK," he said, "we'll try it again soon."

I was relieved. We went back to our quarters, and I was mentally and physically drained. It was one of the most nerve-wracking experiences of my entire life.

The next night, a different group went over to try, all having heard us talking about how tough it was and how much trouble we had had, thus making things all the more tense for them. After about two hours, we heard sirens screaming and fire trucks and ambulances roaring over to the auxiliary field.

"Oh, God!" someone said, "there must be an accident."

We all dashed out to see if we could find out where it was, but no one seemed to know. After a while, however, word came back that one cadet, in trying a solo landing, had flown right into the ground and exploded. They said he must have frozen on the controls. Although we didn't know who he was, we were, by now, all the more shaken up. I'm sure he was dead just as he hit the ground, but because of the flames and heat, of course, they were unable to get him out of the plane, and, as a result, he burned to death. All of us wanted to quit right then. That accident, so close to us, was the very first we had had, and it was a shocker. Later, we learned the cadet who died was Paul Hughes from East Orange, New Jersey. We did not go back for about a week, until everyone had a chance to calm down. But then, we had to resume.

On our second sojourn, there was a moon, making things a little brighter. It didn't seem quite so bad as our first experience. Again, as before, we started with the radio truck on the ground, and about five planes taking off and getting into the landing pattern — with instructors, of course. One at a time, we came in for landings. Each guy was doing a little better. The atmosphere had definitely changed. Maybe out of fear for their own lives, the instructors were doing more instructing now, and there was less screaming, cussing, and yelling. Then, over the radio, a voice announced to all planes,

"OK, you guys, what we are going to do is take you around and land and take off about six times each with your instructors, and then you are going to try it solo. If you give us two good takeoffs and landings solo, we will give you a passing grade. Everybody hear that clear?"

I was sure I had heard it clear, and I was also sure that I was not ready to solo. We went around and made our dual landings, and after six each, they put the question to us all:

"Who is ready to solo?"

Three or four said they were ready, and, sure enough, they did it. My instructor asked me if I thought I could do it.

"No way," I answered promptly. "I need more practice dual."

No use kidding myself. No other phase of flying had left me as unsure of myself as this one. So unsure, as a matter of fact, that I thought I would never be able to master it. I really thought this was going to be the end of the line for me.

To my answer, he said, "Well, we will try it one more night, and if you can't do it, I will have to put it on the report sheet, and you know that usually means you are washed out."

I didn't need to be reminded; I knew only too well what it meant! And the reminder did nothing to raise my spirits. I was dejected; I was depressed; mostly, I was scared of washing out. Still consumed by a tremendous desire to complete this training and get my wings, I did not want to wash out.

Back in my bunk, I lay awake all night, talking to myself, trying to regain my self-confidence. And then, realizing there was only one other thing to do, I started to pray. Through the night, I prayed, and I talked to God. I remembered a passage from the Bible: "I can do all things through Christ, who strengthens me." Those words came back to me from the book I had read earlier. Through the long night, I kept saying the words over and over again, and I could feel myself actually gaining self-confidence.

For the next two days, I continued praying, asking God for strength, repeating those words, and asking Him to please let me be able to think straight so that I could use the knowledge I had and apply it without panicking, which would surely be fatal. I was taken over by my obsession: the knowledge that I had to conquer my fear of blackout landings! For the next two days, I was so obsessed, I could think of little else. My mind was on prayer and God and fear and death and washing out.

In my contemplation, something else from that book I had read came to mind, a quotation from Ralph Waldo Emerson. I thought about it a lot. "If you fear something, get up and do it right now." I was getting myself mentally ready for the test which was soon to come. Desperate, I knew that failure in this one aspect meant I would be out of the Air Force. After about three days, I was pretty well prepared mentally, I thought, although there were lingering doubts because I knew what I was not able to disclose: this was a vision problem. I knew I could fly the plane. I knew I could land the plane. I had no doubts about my flying ability. But I also knew that I had bad depth perception at night, and my distance vision was not good. As I said, I was not about to tell them, but I reasoned that there had to be a way, and I was determined to find it.

When the time came for us to go over again, only three or four of us who were having trouble were there. My instructor and I got into the plane, and we had a little talk; only this time, he was not loud or boisterous. As a matter of fact, he was rather calm and nice.

"I know that you are scared," he said, "and I know how much this means to you. I think you are actually making it harder on yourself by worrying so much. Now I know what kind of a pilot you are; you have done very well up until now, and I would hate to see you wash out now. I have flown with you for several weeks, and I know that you can do it. You have done everything else satisfactorily, and there is no reason why you can't do this. Now your biggest problem is fear. You are scared to death that you are going to fail. Now just go up there, try to relax, and think about what you have to do."

And then he repeated, "I know you can do it!"

Well, I was absolutely shocked — that he would sit there and give me such an inspirational pep talk. That was the very first time in about eight weeks of associating with him that he'd given me any kind of encouragement. It gave me a tremendous lift to think that he, after yelling and cussing at me for so long, told me that he had confidence in me and that he thought I could do it.

"OK, now we are going up together, and we are going to shoot three takeoffs and landings together, and you are going to do it all just as if I weren't in the plane. And then, after that, I am going to get out, and you are going to give me two good solo landings, and then we will go home."

I said, "OK, that's fair enough; let's go." By this time, my mental attitude had improved 100%, what with all the praying I had done, and now especially after the pep talk he had given me. It helped a whole lot.

We taxied out, and I did it all. He was just a passenger. Luckily for me, it was not too dark out. There was a moon. But still, my orientation was not good. Because of my vision, I didn't taxi straight but zig-zagged down the field. When I got to the end of the runway and received clearance to take off, I gave it the gun. From the rear cockpit, where I was located, I had to look over the instructor's head in the front seat. Well, I got to going down the runway crooked. Instead of stopping in the center of the runway, I got up enough speed to take off before I ran off the runway altogether. He did not comment about that at all. I got up in the air and was watching my instruments to stay straight and level. At night, if you can't see the horizon, you have to rely on your instruments because, of course, everything is relative. If you could see the horizon, you could fly level according to it.

I flew around the field and prepared for my first landing. I was afraid. Not so much confused now, as before, but just fearful of not doing well. I said a prayer: "Please, Lord, just let me find those two blue lights, and then I think I will be all right." My instructor was silent, not saying anything. He was just letting me do my thing. I made my final turn to get lined up with the runway. I looked for the blue lights. I couldn't see them! "Lord, where are they?" I prayed. Immediately, I spotted them. I had overshot them, and now I was too high to come in. Realizing that I had turned too quickly, I got on the mike and said,

"Bill, I'm sorry. I overshot. I will go around and try again. Is that OK with you?"

"Yes," came the reply. "Do you know what you did wrong?"

"Yes, I do; I turned too soon."

"That's right. Now, relax."

I went around once again, and this time, I went way beyond where I had turned before, and suddenly, when I did turn, it was very clear; I could spot the blue lights very easily, and I had a longer approach. I got lined up with the runway and, using a combination of instruments and visual, I gradually let down.

I discovered that the longer approach I had, the easier it was to bring it down. But I still had one problem; I could not see the grass field well enough to judge how low I was so that I could set the wheels down gently. To compensate, I felt my way down. I hit the ground pretty hard — twice — and then I let it roll a ways, gave it the gun, and took off again.

All during this time, my instructor was not commenting — just observing, but ready to take the controls in a minute. Finally, he said,

"That was not too bad. Take it around once more, and then I'll let you go alone."

I was shaking! His lack of comment and criticism worried me more than anything. I was used to having him screaming his head off.

I got the idea that, at last, he was trying to help me. Or, perhaps, he just feared for his life, too. I just couldn't believe that I was getting this kind of encouragement from him. I began feeling a sort of responsibility toward him for having faith in me. I felt now that I couldn't let him down. My fears had overwhelmed me to the point that I could not think. If only I could conquer my fear of blackout landings, I felt sure I could think straight and do all right. I knew that, if I were landing on a concrete runway, I would be able to see the light-colored concrete at least a little bit. Just enough, anyway, to tell if I were coming in straight from the air. But to judge distance from the ground on a green grass field was very difficult for me at night. Now we went around again, and this time, I took an even longer approach, simply because I wanted more distance to be able to line myself up with the runway. I was still awaiting a comment from him, but nothing! By now, I was getting more concerned about his silence than about anything else. *He's displeased and ready to give up on me,* I thought.

Turning for my approach, I spotted the blue lights and began descending very carefully. But I was coming in too short. I realized it as I got low to the ground. I gave it some throttle. That took me up a little. Then, afraid I had gone too far, I pulled back the throttle and hit the ground hard again. And then again! The reason, of course, I knew: I just couldn't see the ground.

"OK. Taxi over to the radio truck, and I'll let you go up alone," he said.

I brought the plane to a stop.

He looked at me and said, "Do you feel like you want to try it alone? I am not going to force you to do it. But you know that I will have to make a report, and you know what that means? That means you will probably be washed out."

There was a brief pause, and then he added, "Now, I know you can do it. But it all depends on your own faith in yourself."

I thought for a moment. Then, although I was scared to death — not because I couldn't fly the plane, but because I couldn't see well — I answered,

"Yes. I am going to do it."

"OK," he said, and he climbed out.

His parting words to me as he stepped down: "Just relax and think!"

Alone now, I taxied the plane to the end of the runway, all the time saying to God, "Well, Lord, if I ever needed you, I need you now. Lord, I am putting this whole situation in your hands. I can't do it without you. If it is your will that this is my time to die tonight, well, so be it."

I turned the plane around and pushed the throttle forward. Two blue lights marked the far end of the runway in front of me, and I tried to keep the plane right in the center of those steadily while I gained speed. When I had enough speed, I took off and climbed to altitude by watching my instruments and altimeter, being careful not to climb too fast and stall out. Suddenly, I felt myself in control of the plane! I was flying the plane; it was not flying me.

The night was pitch black. My stomach was empty; I think I had swallowed it. I turned off all of my cockpit lights, so as not to get any glare. I circled the field, and, when I reached the point where I was supposed to turn for my approach, I passed it a bit to make sure I had enough room to get lined up. Then, turning into the runway, I saw the blue lights and began letting down. I dropped the flaps and lowered the air speed, watching my altimeter constantly, as that was the only way I could tell how low, or close to the ground, I was. As I kept cutting the throttle slowly and coming down little by little, I realized that I was finally using my head. I was thinking. Maybe it was because I wasn't worried about what my instructor was thinking. I wasn't just thinking; in fact, I was in deep concentration.

I came down very easy and touched the wheels to the ground fairly well, bouncing a little, but not as much as the first time.

He was on the radio, and he said, "OK, now go around again." I gave it the gun and started to take off, unknowingly heading for the side of the runway once again.

He shouted over the radio, "You are too far over to the right! Get back in the center — quick! And give it throttle!"

I gave it left rudder, got back on course, and got it in the air again.

He was still on the radio. "OK, now come on; land it just like you did before, and then we will quit for tonight."

I came around and landed just like before. Maybe a little worse. Then I taxied over to the radio truck; he climbed back in, and we went back to the main field. When we got back there, and after not one word of conversation on the way back, we parked the plane.

"Well, tell me something," I finally said. "I want your opinion. How did I do? Am I in trouble or what?"

"Well, to tell you the honest truth," he said, "I was not too satisfied with your flying tonight. In all fairness and honesty, I can not give you a very high grade on this performance. You still have a weakness of some kind in your night flying. For your own good, I will have to put that in the report, and chances are, you might get a check ride from the CO. Actually, it will be for your own good; after all, you might kill yourself sometime."

Of course, I knew what my problem was, but I wasn't about to tell him. A few days went by. We continued our routine flying, ground school, Link trainer, and all the rest of our regular daily duties. Then came a notice from Captain Williams, ordering me to report to his office the next morning. I was shaken. All sorts of things went through my mind: *I wonder if he is just going to wash me out right now, or if he is going to give me one more chance. Maybe he isn't going to give me a check ride.*

I didn't sleep much that night. I lay awake worrying, and I said many prayers. Finally, after all the worrying — practically all night — I asked myself, *Why in the heck am I so obsessed with becoming a pilot, anyway?* I thought, *Hell, if they wash me out, I'll probably get an easy desk job someplace and never have to go to combat. So, what the hell — let them wash me out. I don't give a damn. I'm tired of worrying about it.*

The next morning, I reported to Captain Williams' office. He asked me to come in and sit down. He pulled out all of my records dating back from pre-flight to primary and basic and looked them over awhile.

Then he said, "You know, LaHood, your records look pretty satisfactory to me, but I understand that you are having some trouble with night flying. At least that's what it says in this report."

"Yes sir," I said. "I guess I am."

"Do you know what, exactly, it is that is giving you trouble?"

"No," I said, "not exactly." He did not ask about blackout landings, and I wasn't going to volunteer any more information than I needed to.

"Well, it's customary that I take a check ride with a student whenever he is having a problem, so why don't we take a little ride tonight, and we will see what the trouble is."

He still hadn't mentioned anything about blackout landings.

He just said, "Meet me on the flight line tonight at 9:00 p.m."

I was thinking to myself, *If he is planning on just flying from the main field, where we have runway lights and beacons, it will be a snap, because I can fly from a lighted field as well as any student. And my navigation at night is good — I have done a lot of dead reckoning and a lot of radio-beam flying.* So I was not too worried. Unless, of course, he says, "Let's go shoot some blackout landings…"

I reported at 9:00 p.m. that night.

We got into the plane, and he said, "OK, now take off and fly me to Albany, Georgia."

Albany was about 75 miles north of Bainbridge, where we were.

"And then from there, I want you to take me back down to Valdosta, Georgia." Valdosta was southeast from Albany about 70 miles.

"Then take us back home." It was just a big triangle.

I was delighted. He hadn't mentioned anything about blackout landings. *I've got it made now,* I thought. *This is going to be a snap.* I had flown this run a half-dozen times before. I knew the exact heading to take to Albany. I taxied out and got a clearance from the tower. "Please let me do everything right, God," I asked.

I got the first thing right when I got a clearance from the tower. The captain was impressed with that. I gave it the throttle and started down the runway. The captain was a big guy, and he was in the front cockpit, so I had to look over his head. I got flying speed, took off, and climbed to about 5,000 feet until he said,

"OK, level off, and take up a heading to Albany."

I did as I was instructed, and I had my radio beam receiving a signal from the Albany station. I checked the little towns off on the map as I passed over them.

Occasionally he would say, "I'll take the controls a while," and then he would circle around purposely to try to get me lost.

I knew what he was doing, but I kept a close watch on where he turned and where I was. After about 15 minutes, he would give me back the controls to see if I could get back on course. Well, I had no trouble whatsoever, because if I had one thing that I was pretty good at, it was direction finding. I quickly got back on course.

It took about 30 minutes to get to Albany, and when I got over the field, I called in to report who I was and where I was going. When you pass a radio or radar checkpoint or an airport, you usually call in and tell them who you are. For example: "Military aircraft on training flight, two passengers, flying at 5,000 feet, coming from Bainbridge, Georgia, destination Valdosta, estimated time of arrival 10:45 p.m." In case you crash or get lost, they will know what time you passed this point and what time you were supposed to be at your destination, and they will know where to start looking for you.

The captain was pleased about my procedure call, and so I turned and took up a heading to Valdosta. On the way there, he did the same thing once again — took the controls and tried to get me lost. However, I always got back on course, and I reached Valdosta at the right time or close to it and then took up a heading for home. He did several other things to rattle me: told me to turn off radio, fly with no radio, just visual navigation, etc. But all of that was easy for me.

When we got back to our main field, he said, "Now I want you to shoot several landings for me."

That, too, was OK with me, as long as the lights were on.

I came in for the first landing, and it was almost perfect. Then I went around again, and came in again, and it was also a good-enough landing.

Then he said, "OK, make one more — only this time, do not turn your landing lights on."

Landing lights were in the wings, two powerful headlights, similar to headlights on a car, only a lot brighter.

They gave a tremendous amount of light. *Well,* I thought, *that's not too bad, as long as the runway lights are still on.* You wouldn't exactly call that a blackout landing because the runway lights threw an awful lot of light. As I came around, I remembered that I had better take a little longer approach, so I could ease it down. I did. Taking a little longer approach, I brought it in with a little power until I was just about on the ground, and then I cut the engine and made a really nice landing. He didn't say much as I taxied over to the ramp. By then, it was about 11:45 p.m. I was tired and nervous. I stopped the plane, and we got out and started walking back to the flight room. I was anxious to know something, but he wasn't talking.

When we got inside, he sat on the table and said, "Well, I don't see anything too wrong with your flying. Your takeoffs were good. Your navigation was OK. I tried to get you off course, and you got back all right. Your landings were not great, but they were fair. If I were you," he went on, "I would work a little harder on your landings. That last landing, you made just a little too long of an approach. Just go out and work on those things."

I was so glad and so surprised. I wanted to ask, "Do you mean that I'm not washed out?" But I thought I'd better keep my mouth shut.

"I think you'll be all right," he said. "Just work on those things."

Wow! I was born again. This was the greatest day of my life. I knew I could pass the check ride if I didn't have to shoot blackout landings. I knew he could never get me lost on the run to Albany and Valdosta because I had made that run so many times that I could have done it blindfolded. I felt great.

The next day, my instructor asked, "How did it go last night?"

I said, "OK, I guess. He just told me to work on a few things a little more."

My instructor shrugged his shoulders and said, "Good."

And that's all there was ever said about it. But I surely thought for a while that I was going to be out of the Air Force. That was my worst experience while in training.

CHAPTER 4

Advanced Training

In a couple of weeks, we ended our basic training, and I got a passing grade on all phases of flying and ground school. Now we were awaiting our orders and where to report for advanced training, which was the last phase of pilot training. Usually, they split the class in half and sent some to fighter training and some to bomber training. Fighter training means to learn how to fly a single-engine fighter. The training plane they used in fighter training was called an AT-6. It was similar to the basic trainer BT-13 that we had just been flying, only it was faster and had more horsepower — about 650 HP, as compared to 450 in a BT-13. It was also more maneuverable; it had retractable landing gear, while the others didn't. It was equipped with machine-gun sights and cameras. All around, it was a better and faster plane. It also had a narrower wheel base, which made it very tricky to land. When you came in for a landing, you had to be very careful to keep it straight, as it was very easy to ground loop. Ground loop means the plane turns completely around, a 360-degree turn, while rolling down the runway. I believe they must have split our class at random and sent some to fighter school and some to twin engine.

I was chosen to go to twin-engine school. Although, at first, I had my heart set on being a fighter pilot, it really didn't make any difference to me when I was sent to twin engine. I really didn't mind. We got our orders to go to Columbus, Mississippi, for advanced twin-engine training. After I got my orders and before I left, I went to see Bill Martin, my instructor, and I had a nice talk with him. He really wasn't too bad of a guy after it was all over. I thanked him and apologized for giving him so much trouble and told him that I appreciated it that he didn't wash me out. We shook hands; he wished me luck and said, "Maybe we'll meet again sometime."

I was so glad to get out of Bainbridge, Georgia. All the time I was there, I never once went into town; I was always too busy studying. We left the next day by cattle train to Columbus, Mississippi. Columbus was a very little town on the eastern border of Mississippi, right next to Alabama. We arrived there the next morning, and although this was a little hick town, the airfield was quite nice, and the living quarters were much better than those at Bainbridge. At least we had private rooms at Columbus, with two guys to a room, and the rooms were clean.

We did not meet our new instructor the first day, but we did walk down to the flight line to view the new airplane that we were going to be training in. It was the Cessna Bobcat, a twin-engine, four-passenger plane, with two seats in front and two behind the pilot and co-pilot.

It had dual controls, and it had many more instruments than we had ever seen before. I got up and sat in the pilot seat, and it felt very strange. There was so much room, and I was just used to sitting in a small cockpit in a single-engine trainer.

The next day, we met our new instructor. Each instructor had five students. Ours was an elderly gentleman. I don't mean he was old. I imagine he was in his early 40s, and he was a very nice, easy, soft-spoken man. He would talk to us for long periods of time on the ground and explain everything in detail before we would go up and fly. He was a real teacher. The first time he got us five cadets all together, he gave us a little talk. "Boys," he said, "you are all evidently pretty good pilots, or you wouldn't have come this far in your training. You've just finished a very hard part of your training in basic training. But now you are here to learn many more fine points of flying. I am going to teach you to fly a bigger, twin-engine plane, with a lot more sophisticated instruments. We are going to take our time. I am not going to harass you. We are going through every phase of this instruction slowly until you get it down perfectly. There is a lot to learn, and if you will cooperate with me, and be attentive when I tell you something, we will get along well."

He was a tall, slim guy with gray hair, who looked like a real veteran flyer. He never got excited and never moved very fast at any time. He always explained everything very thoroughly. He was a civilian flying instructor, not an Air Force officer. That's probably why he was such a nice, easygoing guy. Air Force officers who are newly commissioned sometimes let the rank go to their head. They are arrogant and cocky.

We started flying the AT-10 the next day, and it was a tremendous experience, insofar as how it felt and handled. And the visibility out the front was so great. You had a wide windshield with nothing obstructing your view, as the engines were in the wings — not like a single-engine plane, where you are looking straight out over that long engine. Although I had my doubts at first about flying a multi-engine plane and had had my heart set on flying a fighter, once I got to flying this twin-engine plane, I just loved it. And besides, it wasn't so lonely, because you had someone else in the cockpit to talk to and to help make decisions.

We had two different kinds of advanced trainers. One was the AT-10, with a conventional landing gear — that is, with two wheels in front and the tail wheel in the rear. The other was the AT-9, which was also a Cessna, but instead of the tail wheel in the rear, it had a nose wheel. This was a much faster plane. You could bring it in for a landing at a higher rate of speed. That, however, was no big deal, for, as our instructor told us at the beginning, we were scheduled to learn many more fine points of flying in this plane. And that we did.

We did not have to do any more aerobatics or spins or any of the earlier maneuvers. It was all instrument flying, radio procedure, navigation, longer trips, a lot of formation flying, a lot of night cross-country. There were many hours of Link trainer and a lot of classroom instruction. We had nobody screaming at us now, and we were beginning to be good Air Force pilots. Every time this instructor took us up, he would sit down and talk about what we were going to do — while we were still on the ground, before we ever took off. He was a real teacher, and I learned more from him than from anyone else.

We began advanced training about March 1, 1943, and it lasted all through April and May. I was enjoying this twin-engine plane more and more all the time; after we had soloed, we were free to just go out and check out a plane any time we were not in ground school and go up and practice — providing, of course, there was a plane available. I did it every chance I had, because I loved it. The weather in Mississippi at that time of year was nice, and I wanted all the hours I could get.

About the middle of our training, they picked about ten of us students at random and told us that we were going to go to Eglin Field, Florida, to fighter training. We couldn't figure it out, and nobody had an explanation. When I asked my commanding officer, he said he didn't know. He said, "You'd just better go, I guess." So, we went down there. They flew us down, and we got attached to a squadron. We had to fly the AT-6, the single-engine plane. I had never flown one before, but as I said earlier, it was much like the BT-13 that we had flown in basic training, only faster and bigger. We flew it around for a few days to get used to it. Then we started gunnery training.

They had machine guns mounted in the wings, and a camera to track the bullets to see if you had hit the target. First, we aimed the plane at a target on the ground and then dove right at the target. There was a gunsight right in front of you, and you put the target right in the gunsight. The machine-gun trigger was right on the control stick that flew the plane, so when you had the target in your sights, you pushed the button, and your machine guns would fire.

If you were on target, you would get some hits; you dove pretty low, pulled up, went around, and did it again. We did this for about an hour a day; then we had to go up and chase a flying target.

They had a plane that would tow a canvas target on a rope or cable about 100 yards behind the plane. We would go up and get higher than the target, as if it were an enemy fighter plane, and then dive at it and shoot at it, and our cameras recorded all of our hits. We did this for about a week or ten days. I didn't like it at all; I wanted to get back to my twin-engine planes. I knew then that I did not want to be a fighter pilot. I went to the CO and told him that I was not happy doing this and that I wanted back to my outfit, as did the other nine guys who had come with me. So, they agreed to send us back. I still don't know why they picked us. However, it was a good experience. At least I knew then that I had no doubt in my mind: I wanted to be a bomber pilot now. I had had a desire to be a fighter pilot and fly a P-47 or P-38. I had the impression that those were the two best and fastest planes in the Air Force. And I guess they were. I was always fascinated by their speed and maneuverability. But, after spending ten days at that fighter-training base, I completely lost interest in those planes and the idea of being a fighter pilot. I got to thinking one day when I was up there chasing that canvas target, *What if I was the one being chased by some more experienced German fighter pilot, and I couldn't get him off my tail? Well, it would be the end for me.* Right then, I decided this was not for me. I wanted to get back to multi-engine planes for a couple of different reasons: I was thinking that, maybe after the war, I could fly a commercial plane for an airline company or a charter plane or something. I would at least have had the experience.

We got back to our regular base and began our twin-engine training once again. Just because this was a twin-engine plane, it did not necessarily require two people to fly it. One pilot could fly it very well. In fact, that is what we did most of the time. I would check out a plane and fly by myself most of the time, unless another student had to practice the same procedures.

While I was in my advanced training, I received a letter from one of my roommates in primary training, John Fogarty. He was stationed at a fighter base somewhere in Louisiana; I think it was Barksdale. He told me that he and Bill Finnegan were still together and that they were taking advanced fighter training. He also told me that our other roommate, Merle Farley, had washed out in basic training and that they had lost track of him. I was very sorry to hear about Farley. I really don't know what he did for the remainder of the war. I'm sure that, whatever he did, he had a lot of fun doing it, because that's the kind of a guy he was — happy-go-lucky. A couple of days later, I decided to fly down and see John and Bill. When I asked if I could check out a plane and take a routine cross-country training flight to Barksdale, it was OK by the CO. So, I went and took another student with me. It was about a two-hour trip one way. When we took off, the weather was beautiful, but the further we went, the cloudier it got. We arrived there about 11:00 a.m. and spent about an hour trying to locate Fogarty and Finnegan. By the time we found out where they lived and got to their quarters, we found out that they had gone on an all-day mission of some kind and wouldn't be back until late. We couldn't wait around because we had to get the plane back, and besides, the weather was beginning to close in, and it was getting dark and windy. We left without seeing them. On the way back, we ran into bad weather. The clouds were rolling and very black, right in the direction that we were going. We were beginning to get very worried, because we had never experienced anything like it before. I wished that I had listened to my meteorology teacher more than I had. One thing I knew for sure, and that was never to fly into a "thunderhead" — a black cloud, very turbulent inside, and capable of ripping a plane all to pieces.

We talked it over and decided to call a weather station in the vicinity and see how we could avoid this storm. We radioed into a station and told them where we were and where we were going. They gave us instructions to get out of the area immediately, change course, and fly due east for at least 50 miles and then north for about another 50 miles. Then, if it was clear, we could head back west and back to our base. We did what they told us, but it was still rough after 50 miles, so we continued on some more until it looked clear. Then we headed north for about an hour. By this time, we had no idea where we were. We were definitely lost. It was then about six o'clock in the evening, and we were getting scared. We could not identify some of the little towns that we flew over on the map. Finally, we had sense enough to follow a railroad track to a large town and found out that we were over Montgomery, Alabama, only about 100 miles off course. We knew how to get back to our field from there. We got back about 8:00 p.m., and we caught plenty of hell from the operations officer. Although we were a little frightened while we were lost, I don't think we actually began to panic. We were able to prove to ourselves that we were beginning to know how to react in a crisis. I think we kept our heads on straight and started to use some of the things we had learned in training.

If there is one thing that you learn and learn well, going through Air Force pilot training, it is how to be organized. You learn to organize your life right from the beginning in pre-flight school, where everything is organized — the way you dress, how you eat, how you attend classes and functions on time, and how you maintain your living quarters. But those are all personal things. Flying an airplane is an altogether different area, but, still, one in which you must be extremely well organized. For example, there are about 50 items listed on a chart that you must check before you even start an engine. This checklist is in the cockpit, and it is checked by you and your co-pilot, so that there is nothing overlooked. There are people's lives depending on you to see that everything is functioning properly. The more complex the plane, the longer the checklist. This is a daily routine before starting engines. There are so many things on an airplane which, if overlooked, not working, or about to malfunction could cause a real disaster. So it's best to keep checking everything all the time. Many planes have crashed, and many people have lost their lives because some person was careless and didn't bother to check things out a little further. Going over a checklist is a must.

We resumed our twin-engine training with a lot of instrument flying and a lot of formation flying. About the final three weeks of our advanced training, we started flying the AT-9 instead of the AT-10. As I said before, it was a faster and more maneuverable plane. We did a lot of night flying now, and we also had to do a good deal of blackout landings. However, I did not fear them quite so much in a twin-engine plane, because the visibility was so much better. You're sitting right up there in front of a large windshield, with no need to strain your neck looking out over a long engine. Our blackout landings at this field were much easier because we used the concrete runway to land on. Although they turned off all the runway lights and all other lights, we could still see the runway very faintly, especially if it was a clear night, as the concrete is light-colored. I had no trouble whatsoever with my landings here. I made some fairly good ones; at least I thought so. And my instructor said I did all right. When we began flying the AT-9, we lost our good civilian instructor, and now we had another Air Force officer for a teacher.

I was sorry to have to change instructors, because I liked the civilian very much, and I learned an awful lot from him. I wish I could remember his name, but I can't. When we started with the officer, all the harassment started all over again. It was fortunate that we had only about three more weeks to fly with him before graduation. I think the purpose for getting him was primarily to learn to fly formation in a faster plane.

The last few weeks, we flew a lot of formation. It was a whole bunch of fun; it required total concentration. You could not take your eyes off the plane next to you; you had to constantly jockey the throttle back and forth to maintain a relative position; you had to be alert every second.

Graduation was coming soon. It was then about the middle of May 1943, and I think graduation was scheduled for May 23rd. Of course, graduation at a military academy is a very formal and traditional extravaganza. Everyone had been preparing for it for weeks in advance. There were to be parades, military aircraft flying exhibits and the usual speeches by generals and colonels and commanders of the bases. And, of course, the long, boring procession of each cadet going up to receive his wings and diploma and also his second lieutenant bars. This all took about an hour. The weather was beautiful, and it was all held outside. There were many friends and relatives and wives and girlfriends of cadets there. However, I did not have a wife or a girlfriend, and I did not want to burden any of my family and ask them to come down to my graduation. So, I was just one of the boys who did not have anyone from home, and there were many of us.

One of the generals made a speech, and he said, among other things, one thing that stuck with me: "Gentlemen, you are now no longer students or cadets. From this moment on, you are full-fledged Air Force flying officers, and you are expected to act like, and assume the duties of, an officer. You are now a leader, and you are expected to accept and assume any assignment the Air Force assigns you." When I heard his statement, I suddenly felt the burden of responsibility on my shoulders. I thought, *Wow! They could send us to Africa or Germany or any place there was combat, and I don't feel anywhere near ready for that yet.* I didn't worry much about it right then, however, because I was so happy to have graduated and received my wings. It was surely one of the greatest days of my life.

That night, there was the graduation ball in the main auditorium. It was a very formal ball, and practically everyone had their wives and girlfriends. Several of us had to go stag. It was no use to go to town to try to meet some girl just to ask her to go to the dance. Anyway, there were not enough girls to go around. We had a nice time anyway, drank our share of highballs, and celebrated until the wee hours of the morning. We were all very proud of those silver wings!

The next day, after all the excitement of graduation and the party had worn off, I began to wonder what they had in store for me. I wondered if I would be going to combat right away or staying here and going to instructor's school. I was very anxious to know something. I didn't have to wait long. The next morning, I got a memorandum telling me to report to Lockbourne Air Base in Columbus, Ohio, to begin transition training in a 4-engine B-17 bomber. *Oh, my God,* I thought, *me — fly a 4-engine bomber? They've got to be kidding! I can hardly handle a twin-engine plane, let alone a 4-engine.*

That was May 25, and I had to be in Columbus, Ohio, on June 1, so I did not have time to go home for a visit. Instead, I hung around for a day and then left for Ohio. They flew us there in a C47 transport plane. Several of my close friends were also being sent there, so I knew a lot of guys.

CHAPTER 5

Transition Training

Lockbourne Air Base was a huge place. We were absolutely awed by the size of the runways and the many bombers lined up. The first thing we did after our arrival was to walk over and look at a B-17 bomber, the plane that we were sent there to learn to fly. I took one look at it from close range and immediately said, "No way can I fly this huge plane!" It was so large I couldn't even believe that it could fly. The cockpit must have been 20 feet up in the air. I kept saying, "I don't believe it. I don't see how I will ever fly this thing." The wheels simply amazed me; they were practically as high as my chest. In 1943, it was the biggest plane that the Air Force had in operation, and it was the best. It was known as the Flying Fortress. It was definitely the most advanced and well-equipped bomber in the United States Air Force. As a matter of fact, it was said many times that the Flying Fortress won the war for the US. Although large, it was a beautiful airplane. To see it take off and land was a thrill. I actually stood there with my mouth wide open, just like a farmer coming to New York for the first time.

The plane was a magnificent sight to behold — such an engineering marvel! A monster of a plane by the standards of the 1930s and 1940s. Many models were built each year, and ever improving, at costs ranging in the millions and billions. Prototypes were junked, many crashed on first flights, but Boeing Aviation continued to construct and test and improve on the B-17 until they came up with the most magnificent flying machine ever built up until that time. It was a thing of beauty. The average cost per plane was $300,000; in 1935, that was a lot of money. The plane had a wingspan of 103 feet, and the length — front to rear — was 68 feet. It weighed 30,000 lbs. empty. When we flew them in combat, the weight was 60,000 lbs. That's 30 tons. It was hard to believe that a thing like that could fly, but I want to tell you that it was the most stable, marvelously constructed, and the smoothest-flying plane that anyone ever flew. It was a dream, and I just fell in love with it the minute I started to fly it.

Our training at Lockbourne Air Base was to be about eight weeks. We began our instructions within a few days after arriving there. My instructor was an Air Force captain, a medium-sized guy and very stocky. I don't recall his name now, but he was a very good man and an excellent teacher. There were four students to one instructor. We began by first learning how to take off and land the huge plane. The cockpit must have had an instrument panel with about 80 or 100 dials and gauges. It was just a mass of instruments with numbers, arrows, lights, etc. I thought I could never — even in a year — learn what they all meant. The plane was equipped with four Pratt and Whitney engines of 2000 HP each. We were used to flying twin-engine planes with two engines of 250 HP each. It had four throttles, all together — so that you grabbed all four at the same time. It was like holding on to a hammer handle. The throttles were in a horizontal position; when you wanted power, you just pushed all four throttles forward at the same time. As you pushed them forward, you felt the tremendous forward thrust of those four 2000-HP engines. The plane had such a huge wingspan that gave it that super-tremendous lift; you had to get it up to only 120 mph to take off. For a big plane, that was terrific. If the plane was empty, it would take off at 110 mph. In combat, we usually had such a heavy load that we would get a little more speed.

For the first week at Lockbourne, we did nothing but short takeoffs and landings, and it was getting easier all the time. As I said before, it was not a hard plane to fly. It was so stable, it was like flying a hotel. In fact, it was so stable that you could bring it in for a landing as slow as 90 mph. In flight, it was the most beautiful sight.

After we learned how to take off and land fairly well, we began to fly formation. We flew formation for hours and hours. We had to get really proficient at formation, because that is what we would be doing in combat all the time. Formation flying was hard; it was tiring; it was total concentration. You had to keep your eyes glued to the plane next to you. You were constantly jockeying the throttles forward or back, depending on how far your leader moved away from you. That was the trick: you had to anticipate. You had to have super-coordination because your feet and hands and eyes were constantly working together. We got so good at flying formation that we could actually get so close to each other that we could tap each other's wing tips. Flying formation at low altitude was altogether different from flying at high altitude, by which I mean 30,000 feet. When you are at high altitude, the air is so thin that the plane does not respond as quickly.

When we first began to fly formation at high altitude, it was the strangest sensation. For example, if you overran the plane you were in formation with and you wanted to drop back a bit, you pulled back the throttle, but nothing happened for about what seemed like two minutes. The plane would continue on, even though you let up on the power. The controls just would not react immediately, due to the atmosphere. So, consequently, you had to be extra alert not to overshoot or drop back. It was altogether a different ball game flying at 30- or 40,000 feet.

To see six or eight planes flying a good, tight formation was a beautiful sight. After a few hours of formation flying, your arms would be sore and the muscles tight, because you had your right hand on the throttles and your left hand on the wheel. Your hands were tense, and you had a tendency to grip them tightly. The more tense you got, the tighter your grip was. Also, your two feet were on the rudders, and when you turned your plane or banked it, you had to turn the wheel and the rudders together. You did not make turns with the wheel alone or the rudder alone. It was both together, and that is where the coordination was so important. In addition to everything else, we flew formation every day.

There were a lot more sophisticated instruments in this plane, and we had to learn to use them all. For instance, they would hang a black curtain over the student's side of the cockpit, so that you could not see out the windows at all. We had to learn to take off by instruments, fly a predetermined flight plan, and also bring the plane in for a landing, still with the curtain over the windows. We did this day after day. The hardest part about instrument flying was to make yourself believe the instruments. The instruments would tell you that your plane was flying level, but your body felt as if you were leaning to one side. You would want to right the plane according to your body instincts. The instruments were always right. In order to fly any kind of long-range plane, a pilot has to be capable of reading instruments well. We simply had to learn because many times we would be flying in overcast, or clouds, or at night, or in storms.

Later, while we were flying in England, every morning that we took off, we took off in fog. Of course, England is noted for fog. We were on instruments until we got to 5- or 10- or 20,000 feet sometimes. We would take off at 30-second intervals, and it's just a miracle that we didn't have more air crashes than we did. Occasionally, while climbing to altitude in the fog, one plane would not see the other in front of him, and his propellers would chew off part of the tail of the one in front of him. That would be just a minor thing, and the plane would just come down and land, unless it was damaged too badly, and then it would crash. But, fortunately, that didn't happen very often. At our field, it happened only a couple of times, and the planes that were damaged managed to get down all right. Because the B-17 was such a stable plane, as I have mentioned earlier, it could fly with a lot of damaged parts. I brought a plane back from a mission with two engines out, in fact.

While we were at Lockbourne Field, we did a lot of flying. We did not have much ground school any more, except time spent reading weather maps, learning aerial maps, a lot of link trainer, and many long day and night cross-country trips. Half of our flying at Lockbourne, I think, was at night, but it was easy. In fact, we even had to fly night formation a few times. I was getting good grades on all forms of my training. They graded us on everything; I loved flying this B-17. Although I was so frightened at first at the size of it, after I got to flying it, it was just as easy as any of the trainers I had flown in school. We were all getting pretty good at flying it. We had been at Lockbourne about four weeks by this time, but there was still so much to learn. We had to learn all the mechanical parts and how each thing operated, as well as the function of every gadget.

Everything on the B-17 worked hydraulically — brakes, wheels, flaps, controls, rudders, ailerons — just everything. They had to because of the force and stress on all parts. The oxygen system was something else. It was extremely important. Without oxygen, you could not live if you were higher than 15,000 feet. You would pass out in a short time.

We had to learn ditching procedures, forced-landing procedures. We had to learn how to make bombing runs using the Norden bombsight which was the most treasured secret in America. Germany always wanted to get her hands on it. And the Germans tried — oh, how they tried. I suppose they got it eventually. We had an explosive device built into the Norden bombsight and also into our radio equipment. If we ever had to force-land in Germany, we were under orders to push the button and blow up the bomb sight and our radio equipment to prevent the Germans from getting them and studying their construction. However, I am sure that somewhere along the line, their intelligence agencies got them. The Norden bombsight was responsible for enabling the American Air Force to stage the famous daylight precision bombing, which, in turn, was mostly responsible for winning the war.

As I have mentioned, I loved the B-17 and was so engrossed in it that I wanted to do and learn everything I could and the best I could. I was so motivated, in fact, that I could think of little else. I hardly ever went to town, even though Columbus, Ohio, was a really nice, lively town. If you did go to town, every bar or hotel lounge would be packed with military and Air Force personnel. You couldn't meet any girls, anyway, unless you knew someone who lived in the town and they introduced you to one. I didn't know anyone, so I just forgot about it. If I did go to town, I'd have a few beers and go to a movie or a stage play and go back to the base. I concentrated on flying this plane. I did not have anything to distract me. I didn't have a girlfriend or a wife back home to worry about, no children, no family problems, no distractions at all. I studied hard, read a lot, and flew all I could.

This plane was supposed to be flown with two pilots. However, there were a lot of times they would allow a student to take a plane up alone to practice landings. But we were not to go away from the area. I flew alone many times to shoot takeoffs and landings. And our instrument training continued. In fact, we flew with that hooded cockpit so much that I thought I would lose my mind. It was so hard and boring. And formation flying was beginning to be a drag, especially when you had two or three hours of it a day. Even though formation flying was tiresome, my instructor told me that I was getting pretty good at it. I had the best grades of his four students.

On the 4th of July, a big Independence Day celebration was being held at the Cleveland Municipal Stadium. I think it was either before or during a baseball game. They wanted a squadron of B-17s to fly in formation over the stadium at a certain time and at a low altitude, and to make two or three runs at it. The CO wanted students to participate, for the experience. There was going to be a squadron of six planes. A colonel was going to lead the squadron. My instructor recommended me to be one of the wingmen. I was flattered, of course. But I was also scared and nervous, worrying if I could fly a good formation. *Well,* I thought, *all the rest of the guys are students, too, so I'm probably just as bad as they are.*

It was either a Saturday or Sunday; the weather was clear and beautiful, not a cloud in the sky. The planes we used were all washed and shiny. I was supposed to be the colonel's right wingman, so I was right up front. Another student was my co-pilot, but I did all the flying. We took off, assembled at about 2000 feet, and flew over to Cleveland. I don't even know how far it was, but it took quite a while. When we got there, we flew around the stadium about six times — around the perimeter and pretty high. Then, when the colonel got the word to come down and make a run, he called us on the radio and said, "OK, close formation a little tighter. We are going down." I could see that the stadium was jam-packed with people — I'd say about 50,000 or 60,000. We swooped down, dove real low, went right over the middle of the oval stadium, pulled up, circled around, and made two more runs. It was a beautiful sight, I guess, from the stadium, and it was quite an experience for us. After we landed back at our base, the colonel praised all of us students for flying a perfect formation.

I was gaining confidence now in this plane. It was amazing how easy it was to fly it, even though it was so big it scared you. Actually, you had to be most careful taxiing it around because of the long wingspan. I was getting a lot of time in the air, and, toward the final weeks of training, we had to make a few 10-hour night cross-country trips. One particular trip we planned was from Columbus to Chicago to Indianapolis to Louisville to Nashville and back to Columbus. The trip was supposed to be 10 or 12 hours. We gassed the plane for that many hours. Three of us were students, and the fourth person was an instructor. We plotted our course and were going to use every kind of navigation aid that we had learned. The instructor was only a passenger.

We took off at 10 o'clock at night, and as soon as we got off the ground, we tried to retract our landing gear, which is the correct thing to do. It wouldn't go up. We had an electrical problem with it. The only other thing we could do was to crank it up by hand, so we started cranking. We cranked and cranked, and one wheel came up, but the other stuck halfway. Then we tried to crank them down, but neither one would move at all. I think the gears were stripped. Now we had a real problem: we couldn't land. We radioed into the tower and told them what had happened, reporting that our landing gear was jammed and wouldn't come down, and that one wheel was part way down, but we couldn't see how far. They put us on hold while they contacted the engineering officer and mechanics.

Soon, they called us. "There is nothing you can do except make a belly landing, but you cannot make it now with your tanks full of gas, and there is no way to release the gas from the tanks. You'll just have to stay up there until you burn up all of your gas. Then call us, and we will prepare the runway for you to make a belly landing."

"Oh, great!" we said. "That's all we need now. We have enough gas to fly for 12 hours and all the time sit up here and sweat it out."

There was no other way, so we decided to go on the trip anyway, assuming that, by the time we got back, our gas would be low. We flew to Chicago and Indianapolis and Louisville and back, but all that time, we were all worried and discussing how we were going to make that belly landing. Even the instructor was worried. He was sweating and wringing his hands all night long because all of the responsibility was more or less on his shoulders, as he was in charge. About 7:00 a.m., we returned to our base and we reported into the tower, saying that we were back and asking if they were ready for us to belly land. They called back and asked, "How much gas do you have left in your tanks?" As close as we could figure, we had a little less than a quarter of a tank. But, of course, that meant a quarter in each of two tanks, because there is a tank in each wing. We just had our main tanks filled when we left — approximately 1200 gallons. Had we filled our auxiliary tanks in the wing tips also, we would have had a capacity of 2700 gallons. Fortunately, we hadn't; carrying 1200 gallons was bad enough.

The tower told us that it was still too dangerous to try to land with that much gas and instructed us to just fly around the field until our tanks were empty and then to come down. We flew around the field until 9:30 a.m. They must have had a news broadcast on the radio about an airplane in trouble at the air base and preparing to make a crash landing. Several cars were parked along the road near the air field with people out of their cars, standing and waiting to see the crash. The runway was cleared for us. Fire trucks, police cars, ambulances, and rescue outfits were all lined up alongside the runway. The rescue squad were wearing fireproof suits.

We decided how we were going to land. The instructor was in the pilot seat, and he asked me to sit in the co-pilot seat. The other two guys were to sit with their back against the radio-room wall and brace themselves well. When we were almost on the ground, I was supposed to cut all switches, electrical systems, motors, etc.

We had a 5000-foot runway to land on. When we thought the gas tanks were empty, we came down, turned, and lined up with the runway. When we were about 50 feet off the ground, I cut the motors and all other switches. We kept coming down, and it was the loudest noise you have ever heard. The bottom of the plane scraped the concrete runway, and the four propeller blades mounted on the plane's engines hit the ground and bent in half. The ball turret underneath the plane just disintegrated, and sparks flew all over the place. I thought, for a moment, that we were blowing up. We skidded three-fourths of the length of the runway, and the moment the plane came to a stop, the rescue squad ripped the door off the plane and dashed in and pulled us all out. Of course, that's just routine. They do that in case a plane should catch on fire. But we knew that this plane was not about to catch fire. In fact, the instructor and I just felt like sitting there in the seat for a while because we were so relieved to be on the ground. The newspaper photographers were there taking pictures, and the story was in all of the local papers the next day and also on the radio news broadcasts. There was even a small article in the Peoria newspaper about it, with my name, reporting that I had crashed a plane while in training. It was quite an experience. We learned a lot from it, and it made us realize that these malfunctions can occur at any time. It helped us to realize that we should be prepared to meet these problems, be able to think clearly, and not to push the panic button right away. There is usually always a way to handle a situation, providing you can keep your head.

Flying the B-17 was such a gratifying feeling — to think that you had this big thing under control, that you

Lockbourne Air Base – Columbus, Ohio.
June 1943

Minneapolis Airman Safe in Fort Crash

COLUMBUS, OHIO— (U.P.) —A Flying Fortress circled over Lockbourne air base Saturday while its crew attempted for eight unsuccessful hours to free its jammed landing gear.

Finally, its gasoline running low, the plane came in for a belly landing and came to a stop after only slight damage.

Aboard the ship was Lieutenant Louis Lahood, Minneapolis.

Newspaper coverage of training accident at Lockbourne Air Base
1943

were flying it, and it was not flying you. It was a tremendous pleasure to look out of the cockpit windows and see those four engines just purring so gracefully. You could always tell immediately if one engine was not running right or smoothly. It would not be synchronized with the others, and you could detect that instantly. If you happened to be on a trip and you had one engine that had a problem — maybe a burned-out rod or an oil leak that forced you to turn off the engine before you incurred further damage — it would not make any difference at all, because that plane would fly just as well on three engines as it would on four. Even in combat, many times we returned from a mission with an engine out and had to try to stay in formation nevertheless, or get picked off by German fighter planes if we dropped back and flew alone. When you are in formation with 50 or 100 bombers, the Germans would rather not pick on you because you because you have a lot of firepower to shoot back at them. Each bomber had ten 50-caliber machine guns. Multiply that by 100 planes, and that's how many guns a fighter plane would have to face.

We continued our training at Lockbourne Air Base for about another month and were getting to be really good bomber pilots. We were second lieutenants and classified as first pilots. In other words, when our training was complete, we were told that we would be commanding a B-17, that we would have a co-pilot assigned to us, and be issued a plane of our own to prepare for combat. The last four weeks was very technical training and much specialized instrument training, as well as variations of special techniques. In other words, just right down to the nitty-gritty of the fine points of handling and flying this plane. When we finally did finish this transition course, we were classified as Class 1 B-17 bomber pilots. Class 1 meant that the man had had all the instruction needed and was expected to be a proficient Air Force flying officer.

CHAPTER 6

Assignment

I was beginning to get worried. It was, by now, the end of July or the first of August 1943. The Japanese war was going strong in the islands, and I was afraid that they were going to send me there. I dreaded the thought of going over there. However, I found out that they were not yet using B-17s in that theater of operation. But I knew they were being used in Europe. I thought that would be a little better.

After I finished my training at Lockbourne, I received orders to report to a place called Eufrata, Washington, where I was to receive a new B-17 of my own and get a crew assigned to me. Eufrata was close to Spokane and was another hellhole of creation. I got there and did absolutely nothing for a week. I just sat in my room and read, or went to town and drank beer at the one tavern in the entire town of about 800 population — and twice as many servicemen. Finally, one day, I received a memorandum saying: "Your crew will be arriving soon. You will train them and prepare for your trip to England. You will fly your own plane and crew to England to join the US Eighth Air Force there."

I almost fainted. I can't explain the nervous anxiety that I experienced at that moment. *They must be crazy!* I thought. *Here I am, a 24-year-old kid with only 8 weeks and about 200 hours of flying time in this plane, and they want me to fly it across the ocean to England. They have got to be out of their minds! A plane that costs close to a half-million dollars. They've got to be kidding!* I began preparing myself mentally again, and after a while, I got accustomed to the idea, using those ten magic words, the words that had gotten me through so many anxious moments: "I can do all things through Christ, who strengthens me." Soon I began to feel that I was capable of flying it across.

The next day, a nice young fellow came to my room and introduced himself to me. His name was Joe Stoiber, and he was from Milwaukee, Wisconsin — a good, clean-cut boy. He said, "I have just been assigned to you as your co-pilot." I was delighted because he looked like he was going to be very capable. We talked for hours. He had never flown a B-17 before, so I had to take him up every day and familiarize him with the procedure. He had just graduated from flying school. We got along very well, and he was getting to fly the plane very well. We practiced formation flying a lot. We both remarked many times that, since we were going to have to fly our own plane over to England, we hoped to God they'd send us a good navigator. We no sooner got the words out of our mouths when there came a very faint knock at the door of my room. "I wonder who that could be," I said as I walked over to open the door. I opened the door, and there stood a little boy. For a moment, we looked at each other without speaking. I assumed that he was some little kid wanting to sell me a newspaper or something, as he was carrying a briefcase with several sheets of paper. I was a little puzzled, however, and I remember wondering, *Why would a little newsboy be wearing an Air Force officer's uniform?* And, incidentally, the uniform was brand new and a size too large for him. His sleeves almost covered his hands, and his officer's cap fit loosely on his head and touched his ears. *Oh, well,* I thought, *the kid is probably wearing his father's uniform.* Finally, after a moment or two of complete silence while we observed each other, he finally spoke: "Are you Lieutenant LaHood?"

"Yes, I am," I answered.

"My name is Homer Glass," he said, "and I have just been assigned to you as your navigator…"

I froze in my tracks! My heart stopped beating, I think, for a moment, and I turned pale as a sheet. My stomach suddenly had an empty feeling. I thought to myself, *No, God — this can't be true. How can You do this to me?* I looked at Joe, and he looked at me, and we both had a sick look on our faces, I am sure. "I have been looking for your building all morning," Homer went on, "and I finally found you."

Good grief! I thought to myself. *If he couldn't find my room for half a day, I wonder how he is going to navigate us to England.* Oh, Lord, I was sick to my stomach! I invited Homer to come in and meet Joe, our co-pilot.

Homer had a little round baby face and white-blond thin hair. He spoke in a rather high-pitched voice and was very articulate in his speaking. He pronounced his words very distinctly and chose his words very carefully, always trying to express himself very clearly. I began to question him to find out where he had obtained his navigational training and what and how he learned, and what methods they used. Well, he had all the answers. And he had much more, besides, than I had known anything about. I began then to feel that perhaps he was not going to be so bad after all. After we got to flying together, I began to realize how really good he was. Homer was an excellent navigator and a very smart boy. He was a perfectionist, and, later, I had all the confidence in the world in him. He was only 20 years old, I believe, or maybe 21, and he looked no more than 15. I don't believe he had even started to shave the fuzz off his face. Later on, as we began to fly together more and more, I liked him very much. And I still do. He and his wife, Audrey, live in Chicago, and they come to visit us at least once a year. They love to stay at our cottage. They are two of our greatest friends.

In the next few days, we acquired a few more fellows who were to be on my crew. We got a farmer boy from Iowa by the name of Bob Megchelsen, who stood about 6'3" and was kind of slim. He was the tallest one of us all. Although there was hardly enough room in the tail for his lanky legs, he wanted desperately to be the tail gunner. That's the job he wanted, so I gave it to him. He was a wonderful kid, real sincere, and very witty and comical. He provided all the entertainment for the rest of the crew.

For a radio operator, we got Norman Mansfield, from Chattanooga, Tennessee. We had fun razzing him about his southern accent. We got two waist gunners, Ernest Ellington, from North Carolina, and another whose name escapes me now. We got a flight engineer by the name of John Anding, from Oregon. His duties were to see that all equipment was in working order and maintained. We also got a really swell guy by the name of Gail Garner.

Gail and I were the old guys on the crew. We were the same age and had just turned 24 in June 1943. Gail became the leader among the noncommissioned crew. He insisted that he wanted to fly in the ball turret, the bubble on the underside of the fuselage. Two 50-caliber machine guns were housed in the turret, and the turret, itself, rotated, thus enabling the gunner to shoot in any direction at enemy planes below us. There was hardly enough room in the darned thing for an average-sized man, and the gunner had to be curled up in there all day. I'll tell you one thing: You had to have a lot of guts to get into one of those turrets. Well, Gail was never short on guts. He had more nerve than any of us. He was a prince of a guy, good-hearted, and willing to do anything for anybody. He and his wife, Clemmie, have been our very good friends all these years, and we have visited each other many times. Unfortunately, Gail had a heart attack and passed away in 1975. He was only 56. We miss him now, very much.

Except for a bombardier, our crew was, by now, almost complete. Even though we were short one man, we began practicing and flying together. Then came orders to take our plane and crew and move to Kearney, Nebraska, where we were supposed to fly simulated bombing runs. At Kearney, a bombardier named Manuel Cantor joined our crew. After we made the move and got settled down in Kearney, we began to work as a team.

We would be given a certain target for the day, a load of sandbags for bombs, and then we were sent to make our bomb runs and try to drop on our target. The targets were marked on the ground, usually as a white circle. We were very disorganized, and we had poor results. There was a lot of arguing and bickering between Homer Glass, the navigator, and Cantor, the bombardier. They just couldn't get along and constantly blamed each other for the poor bombing results. In fact, no one on the crew had much use for Cantor. He was just one of those obnoxious people you sometimes meet. Nevertheless, we continued practicing bombing missions for at least a month and were, by now, beginning to get used to each other. Everyone was getting to perform their respective duties pretty well.

We were still at Kearney, Nebraska. It was now around October, and we were informed that it wouldn't be too much longer before we would be going overseas. We continued what we had been doing, flying every day, dropping sandbags, and trying to hit the target. The guys complained to me so much about the dumb bombardier who had been assigned to us that I finally got tired of hearing it. I went to the commanding officer, told him that I was tired of hearing all this bitching, explained that we didn't have much harmony on the plane, and said that I wanted a different guy. The commanding officer shipped Cantor out and gave me another bombardier. I can't remember the name of the replacement. However, he was only our second one. By the time we got to England and before we had finished our missions, we had two more different ones. It seemed as if they were all stupid. In fact, everyone in the Air Force calls bombardiers "toggeliers." And that's all they are. The label comes from a function they perform. When a group of bombers go on a mission in formation, the leader — who is usually a pretty high-ranking officer and a veteran bombardier — is the only one who uses the bombsight. He zeroes in on the target, and, when he drops his bombs, all the other bombardiers in the other planes just hit a toggle switch and drop their bombs. That's called "precision bombing." When there are 200 or 300 bombers on one target, each carrying 10 bombs, and all drop together, you see how much damage can be done. And that's exactly how the Eighth Air Force flattened the whole country of Germany.

But back to Kearney, Nebraska. We were still practicing and getting along better with our new bombardier. One day, I was very surprised to get a phone call from my sister Alice. She and her husband Eddie were in Kearney; they had made the trip to come and visit me before I was sent overseas. I thought that was really nice of them, because I had not been home, nor had I seen any of my family since the time I had entered the Air Force. I had not gotten home even after graduation. We had a very nice visit together and went out a couple of nights to some nightclubs. I think they stayed one or two days. It was a nice surprise. I was glad to see someone from home before going overseas. Alice got a kick out of meeting the boys on my crew. She never could get over how small and young Homer Glass was. She said, "He looks like he should still be in grade school!"

I said, "Alice, please don't worry me any more than I am right now. I'm expecting him to get us to England."

We resumed our training flights, trying to get all of the guys accustomed to what their specific duties were. I began to notice, each day as we were flying, that I was having some slight pains in my stomach. However, I didn't worry much about it at the beginning. The pains seemed to come and go at certain times of the day. They began to get progressively worse, though, and I noticed that each time I had them, they lasted a little longer than the time before. I would go up to fly a practice mission for a couple of hours, and, sometimes, I would actually be doubled up, or I would wake up in the middle of the night and have severe stomach pains. I couldn't figure out what was happening to me. Sometimes I would be up all night. The pain would start in my stomach and go all around to my ribs and back. The only thing I could think to do was to take aspirin, and I took them by the dozens. Sometimes at night, when the pain came on, I'd go out to the shower room and take a hot, steaming shower. Occasionally, it would help a little. I wasn't getting much sleep, what with the pain and the fact that I had to be up very early and get to the flight line by 6:00 a.m. to start our flying. Many a morning, I told Joe, my co-pilot, to go down and tell them that I was sick and couldn't come down.

Just about every day, I went to the infirmary and told the doctors that I had stomach pains. But they didn't know what could be wrong with me, and, for that matter, I don't think they even believed me. It was close to the time for us to be leaving for overseas, and a lot of guys were going in with a lot of little ailments, trying to get out of going. But I was really sick. And I kept telling this doctor that I couldn't concentrate on flying at times. I said, "There must be something you can do for me."

"Keep taking aspirin," he said.

All the time, the aspirin was doing more damage to my stomach than helping, but I didn't realize that, of course, and I was taking too many. The doctors in the infirmary were suspicious of all these ailments. I just knew that they thought I was trying to get out of going overseas. Actually, I was afraid that if I went in there too often, they might make me stay or put me in the hospital. Two days before we were ready to leave Kearney, I was in so much pain that I just had to go in. Once again, I saw the same doctor who, incidentally, happened to be the same rank as me, a second lieutenant. When he saw me come in, he said, "Oh, you again."

I was so sick and mad, I shot back, "Listen, you dumb bastard. I have something wrong with me, and you had better try to find out what my problem is." Once again, he examined me, and, after he had finished, he said, "Well, I'll tape your ribs up. I think you might have a touch of pleurisy." He wrapped adhesive tape all around my chest and stomach and then said, "You come back tomorrow for a consultation with this group of doctors." This group were the ones who decided, I believe, who really are too sick to go overseas. Believing that, I did not show up the next day for any consultation, because I was afraid that they wouldn't let me go. I did not want to let my crew down, so I said, "The heck with it! I'll try to live with the pain." If I had only known what it was, I could have done something on my own — go on a diet, drink milk — something.

We packed all of our gear, loaded our planes, and we were ready to leave Kearney, Nebraska, the next day.

CHAPTER 7

Farewell Salute to Home

For some reason I do not know, we had to go to Sioux City, Iowa, for a few days. About 20 B-17 bombers and crews were going to make the trip together. All of us were ready; each of us had our personal belongings in two duffle bags. Our plane was really loaded down. We took off and flew to Sioux City, Iowa, where we stayed for a few days getting more supplies or something. While we were killing time there, I thought, *This is not very far from Minneapolis. What the heck! Why don't I fly up there and fly over my old homestead before I go across?* I gathered my crew; we took out our plane, and I told them that we were going on a routine practice flight. Minneapolis was only about an hour and a half flying time away. I can't remember now whether I called them on the phone at home to tell them that I was going to fly over the house.

We took off and headed for Minneapolis. When I got over the town, I spotted the big gas tank on the corner of Broadway and Central Avenue, and then I knew exactly where I was — headed right for our old neighborhood. Although you are not allowed to fly below 1000 feet over any town, I let the plane go down lower, lower, lower. I spotted our house and I dove right at it, going about 200 mph. I don't think I was 50 feet over the top of the house. We could see the people on the ground, just staring in amazement. I pulled up, circled around, and made another dive at the house. I could see a woman walking down the street toward our house, and, later on, I found out that it was my mother.

When I got back to Iowa, I phoned them and asked if they knew it was me. Of course, they did, and they said that everybody in the area said that their windows had rattled so loudly that they thought they would break. Betty Kourie told me later that she knew that was me and asked, "Did you see me waving my broom?" She lived up on Buchanan Street at the time, about four blocks away from our home. It was a lot of fun!

CHAPTER 8

East to Debarkation Center

Next day, we received our orders to pack up and get ready to leave. Our itinerary was to fly non-stop from Sioux City to Syracuse, New York, land there, and stay overnight. Don't ask me why. But that's what we did. Next day, we flew to Bangor, Maine, which was the debarkation center for the Air Force. There we were to be processed, get all of our immunization shots, and be issued equipment. They issued us so much unnecessary equipment such as handguns, bayonets, machetes — jungle stuff — that we began to wonder if they had changed their plans and were going to send us to one of the islands. After having stayed overnight at Syracuse, New York, we arrived at Bangor, Maine, on December 11, 1943. The snow in Maine was a foot deep all over, and the weather was very cold. The runways, of course, had been cleaned off. My stomach was not hurting so badly on this trip; I suppose I was too busy to think about it.

Twenty B-17s landed at Bangor, and, as we did not fly formation to this place, we all arrived at different times. Bangor had enough facilities to process only twenty crews at a time. That's actually 200 guys, as there are ten men to each plane.

The first day, it seemed that all we did was stand in line to get shots in the arms — sometimes two at once, one in each arm at the same time. They loaded down our planes with supplies for the American troops who were already in England, figuring that, as long as all those planes were going over, they would take advantage of the opportunity to transport supplies with us. Our planes were already loaded down with the personal belongings of each crew member, and, in addition, we had a maximum load of gasoline, 2700 gallons — a lot of weight in itself. In my plane, for example, they put 50 or 75 cases of C-Rations to be delivered to the infantry, I guess. They didn't give me specific instructions about their delivery once I got to England. "Someone there will know what to do with them," they said. In addition to the C-Rations, they put in several cases of cigarettes and, I think, candy. However, the C-Rations weighed the most. I estimated the weight of each case to be about 30 lbs. So all of those cases totaled roughly 1500 lbs. They packed them in the bomb bay, where we normally carry bombs. They were placed right on the bomb bay doors. I would say that we had a maximum weight load.

The following day, they briefed us, showed us the course to fly, and the altitude. We were not going directly to England but instead to a little town in Ireland called Prestwick. Our flying time from Bangor, Maine, to Prestwick would be approximately ten hours. On December 13, we started taking off in about five- or ten-minute intervals.

CHAPTER 9

Destination Ireland

It was starting to snow a little that morning, and although there was a foot of snow all over, the runways were cleared off. About 11:30 a.m., my turn came for takeoff. I taxied out to the end of the runway, praying silently. I was worried that my motors were not warmed up enough to get us off the ground with our heavy load. I prayed over that, and I prayed for all four engines to stay running at least until I got up in the air. When I received the signal to go, I gave the plane all the throttle I could. There was complete silence in the plane. Every guy was tense. I got it rolling as fast as it would go on the ground before I began running out of runway; and then, at about 120 mph takeoff speed, I pulled it up. I kept the throttles all the way forward, and the plane took off beautifully. I kept climbing at about 500 feet per minute, a normal rate, until I got to my prescribed altitude at 9000 feet, and, all the time, I was on our heading. When we got to 9000 feet, we leveled off, and everything was going pretty well. We began to relax a bit, and all of the boys were talking a little once again. Soon, however, we noticed that it was beginning to snow a little harder.

I can't quite explain the feeling you have when you look down at that ocean and there is nothing but water. You are up there and committed. You either do it, or you don't. The vastness of the ocean is frightening when, as far as you can see, there is nothing but water, and for hours and hours. I was not as concerned with what was beneath us as I was with my four engines. My main concern was to keep them running. I knew we would probably make it all right, providing we did not have a mechanical failure. And, of course, the weather was beginning to be a big factor. We were still able to communicate by radio with the Bangor weather station, and we also had inter-plane communication. By that, I mean that we could hear what the planes ahead of us were reporting as far as weather conditions were concerned. And the reports were not good.

The planes that were 20 minutes ahead of us were reporting blinding snow and high wind velocity. Bangor Airport instructed us not to turn back to Bangor. If we could not continue, we were to land at Newfoundland, which was about 200 miles off the coast of Maine. I continued to listen to what the lead planes were doing, and I got the impression that we would all have to land there.

My outside thermometer was registering 45 degrees below zero. Our wings were icing up pretty badly, and I had the de-icers working really hard. De-icers are a rubber tube on the front edge of the wings across their entire length. The rubber tube is the same thickness as the wing; in fact, it is just part of the wing. In other words, the leading edge of the wing was rubber. But inside of this was a terrific air-pressure system that would inflate and deflate that de-icer so that, when ice formed on the front of the wing, the inflation and deflation broke up the ice, and the wind blew it off.

At Newfoundland, which is a province of Canada, I believe, the United States Air Force had a huge Air Force base called Gander Air Base. By now, it had become increasingly evident that we could no longer continue under these weather conditions, so everyone was landing at Gander. We dropped down from 9000 feet to a very low altitude, as the visibility was very bad. Despite the poor visibility, however, we had no trouble finding Gander. But there were so many planes trying to get landing instructions that it was just utter confusion on the radio. They took our calls one by one and stacked us in the traffic pattern. I know that I flew in the traffic pattern for at least 45 minutes or an hour before we got landing instructions.

Trying to find enough room to park all of those huge bombers created much congestion on the field. There were 20 in our group, and there must have been twice that many on the ground from the day before or even the week before. Tractors and snowplows were working feverishly to clear the snow and make room for more planes. Finally, I got the OK to land.

When we got down, we were amazed to see how deep the snow was on the ground away from the cleared runways — two to three feet deep. And those big tractors were trying to move planes and more snow. It was a big mess. But there was nothing anyone could do. When we parked our plane, we had to tie it down to the mooring hooks in the ground to keep it from being flipped over on its back by the violent winds, which did overturn several planes.

Barracks and hotels and just any old empty buildings there were full of Air Force guys. They had to feed us three meals a day. A lot of civilian people were there, working for the government, I suppose. Believe it or not, we stayed there for ten days; that's how bad the weather was. Nobody could fly out of there. All we did was sit around playing poker. We played all day long, stopping only long enough to eat. While I was there, I won a total of $600 or more. I sent home a check for $600 to my sister, Kate, to put into a bank account for me.

After ten days, the weather finally broke a little. There were no more accommodations. They had to get rid of some of us. So on December 23, at 11:30 at night, they called our group and told us to get ready to leave and to meet in the briefing room — pronto. We gathered up most of our personal gear — most of it was still in the plane — and went to the briefing room.

The briefing room is where you're told your prescribed altitude, heading, destination, weather conditions, ETD (estimated time of departure), and ETA (estimated time of arrival). You also learn which radio channel to use, and so forth. Here they remind you of many procedural things that you need to be constantly aware of: "Be sure to check all of your oil-pressure gauges. If your oil pressure begins to drop, you might be going to have an engine problem. Be sure to check your fuel-line-selector switches. Make darned sure your shutoff valve between your auxiliary tanks and your main tanks is open." You see, most of the time, you use only your main gas tanks, which are located in the wings, close to the fuselage. But when you are on a long trip, you also use your auxiliary tanks; they are located way out at the tip of the wings, and they feed into the main gas tanks by gravity — there is no fuel pump that pumps it out. Consequently, if you do not leave the valve open — especially in cold, below-zero weather — the gas line will freeze, or the valve will freeze. Then, when you want more gas in the main tanks, you may be out of luck. When all gas tanks are filled, you have a capacity of 2700 gallons. I don't remember what kind of a range that amount of gas would give you in miles. However, I think it is approximately 10 hours of flying time, or maybe a little more.

The briefing was over in about 45 minutes, and we all had our altitudes. I think they stacked us at different altitudes because there was not very good visibility. My altitude was to be 13,000 feet, and we were going to have to be on oxygen. It was very cold outside — well below zero — there was much snow on the ground, and the runways were just a mass of packed snow and ice. We had so many clothes on, it was ridiculous. We were wearing those all-leather flying suits that had a wool lining and leather boots with that same thick wool lining. They were nice and warm but very cumbersome. They were fine for the guys in the rear of the plane, because there was no heat back there. But we had heat in the cockpit, and, boy, it wasn't long before I started peeling off some of those clothes.

CHAPTER 10

Night Flight Over the Ocean

Our destination was the same as before, Prestwick, Ireland — approximate flying time, 8 hours. If you had a good tailwind, you might cut it to 7 hours. Going from west to east, especially in the northeastern hemisphere, you always have a tailwind, the "prevailing westerlies."

By the time I taxied out to the end of the runway, it was 12:30 a.m. Before taxiing out, I had had my engines running for about 20 minutes. And then, to make sure they were well warmed up, I sat there for about another 15 minutes. The runway we were using was more than 5000 feet long — maybe 6000 — but there was a hangar a couple of hundred feet past the end of the runway, and every plane that took off was having a time clearing that hangar, because the traction was slippery. I was scared to death. I worried about getting this plane off the ground. It weighed 60,000 lbs. — 30 tons. I was worried, too, about my night flying. *Oh,* I thought, *if my basic training instructor could see me now.* And I was worried about the ocean and the weather. I had a million things going through my mind right at that moment. The thought kept passing through my mind, *How stupid of the Air Force to let young, inexperienced kids like us fly these expensive planes and supplies across the ocean!* However, whatever I thought didn't amount to a hill of beans. Right now, the only thing to be concerned with was getting off the ground.

As before, all of the crew were as silent as church mice. I am sure they were more afraid than I was. They were depending on my ability to get them over there safely, and I was determined to try to do it. Homer had told me before we took off that he was going to have to navigate by celestial navigation, providing it was clear enough to see the stars. "Homer, please don't tell me your troubles," I said. "I've got enough of my own." I was just kidding him, of course. I wanted to know exactly how and what method he would use to keep us on course.

We got the signal to go. I turned the plane, lined up to the runway, and gave it all four throttles — slowly, because it was slipping. Gradually, we started to pick up speed as I gave it full throttle. I used the entire runway before I reached 120 mph speed, and then I pulled it up, and we cleared the hangar nicely. We all breathed a sigh of relief! We were off and climbing.

It was a beautiful clear night, the visibility was very good, and we could see the lights on a plane ahead of us. We relaxed a little, and, more for freedom of movement than anything else, I started shedding clothes. We took up our heading and began climbing to our altitude. After we passed 10,000 feet, we had to put on our oxygen masks. It took about a half hour to get to 13,000 feet. The motors were running smoothly, everything was fine, and we were talking to the other planes on the radio. We were beginning to have some fun. Well, I thought, maybe it won't be so bad after all. The one hard part — taking off — is over. Now all we have to do is keep it running, and it will be OK. My eyes were glued to the instruments, temperature gauges, oil gauges, pressure, fuel, oxygen, everything.

Before long, we began hitting rough weather. It was snowing again, and the plane was being bounced around pretty hard. I started to worry again. I called in to see if I could get another altitude to fly and was given the OK to go up to try to get above the turbulence. I climbed and climbed but couldn't break out into the clear; I finally had to level off at 17,000 feet on orders not to go any higher, as they assumed we would soon get through the rough weather. Homer called me on the intercom to say that he could see a clear sky every once in a while, just long enough to use his sextant. (A sextant is an instrument used for measuring angles between stars in order to get a fix on position.)

After a few more minutes, Homer called me back and said, "Take a correction of 20 degrees to the left."

"OK," I said, and we flew for a while on that heading. Now we were picking up ice on the wings, so I was using the de-icer.

Soon Homer called again. "Correct 20 degrees to the left again."

"OK," I agreed. The low visibility was breaking up a little, but nonetheless, I was still scared to death, and I didn't know if Homer knew what the heck he was doing. I was nervous, and Joe, my co-pilot, was nervous. I'm not sure, but I think he was saying a rosary. I'd have been saying one, too, had I not had my hands full. The boys were talking and kidding around on the intercom and laughing, making me all the more nervous, until I finally ordered, "All right, everybody shut up! And don't get on the intercom anymore."

As the weather seemed to be breaking up a bit, I decided to take a lower altitude to get off the oxygen. Flying with that mask on all the time is irritating. I dropped down to below 10,000 feet, and we took the masks off. That was a relief. The weather seemed no worse down there. Shortly, Homer called and said, "Correct 20 degrees to the left again."

"What?!" I said. "Are you sure?"

"Yes. Do it," Homer said.

So, I did. It was now about 2:30 a.m.; we still hadn't seen the water because of being in the clouds all night. Unless there had been a bright moon, we may not have been able to see it even under clear conditions, perhaps. At any rate, I was maintaining a good cruising air speed of 175 mph, the best speed for conserving fuel. Before long, Homer called again, and again said, "Correct 20 degrees to the left."

Right then, I was convinced that Homer was nuts and that we were lost. I was frantic. I called him back and said, "Homer! You dummy! What the hell are you doing? I can just see us going around in a big circle. Are you crazy?"

"No, I'm not crazy," he said. "You correct this plane right now!"

"OK, Homer," I said. "You're the navigator."

What I didn't realize at the time was that we had a terrific crosswind from the north blowing us off course; Homer, standing up in his little hatch with his sextant all night long, was making the corrections. He did a super job.

About 3:30 or 4:00 a.m., I noticed that my air speed was going down. Although I had the same power on, it was dropping … 170 … then 165. I couldn't figure out why, and, for a minute, I panicked. Soon the plane was beginning to mush along. Finally, it dawned on me. Because we were using up a lot of gas out of our tanks, the front of the plane was becoming lighter as the center of gravity changed. That meant there was only one thing to do: in order to get more air speed, we would have to lighten the back of the plane. Instantly, I thought of those 75 cases of C-Rations in the bomb bay. Well, I thought, it's either get rid of those or take a chance of running out of gas. It didn't take me long to decide. I called the crew on the intercom, "Stay clear of the bomb bay because the C-Rations are going." And, with that, I opened the bomb-bay doors and dropped the rations into the ocean. Instantly, the plane leveled out, and our air speed rose. In fact, it went up to more than 175 mph, and I had to let off the throttles a bit.

By now, we had reached the point of no return and had long since passed the point of radio communication with Gander Air Base. We were completely on our own. It was do or die. And I felt sure that we were lost. It's a funny feeling when you commit yourself to flying across the ocean. You have to go through with it — or else. In case of an emergency, there are no airfields or towns or any place to set down. Beyond the range of Gander Air Base, we had only plane-to-plane communication, which made it possible to talk to each other.

Out there, beyond the point of no return, one of our planes was in trouble. Lieutenant Craig, its pilot, from some small town in Arkansas, must not have been listening when they reminded us about that gas-transfer valve. He had forgotten to leave the valve open, as he was supposed to do, in order to allow the gas to run out of the auxiliary tanks. When it came time for him to get more gas into the main tanks, either the gas line or valve was frozen. We could hear him desperately trying to reach Gander Air Base's air rescue station, trying to radio them his approximate location. We all knew their chances of making contact with Gander were not good. In fact, it was practically impossible, because they were too far out. I don't think they ever got a response, even though they tried and tried frantically to reach someone. Even had they gotten a response, it would have taken the air/sea rescue crews forever to find them at night.

"We are going down!" they kept screaming on the radio. "We need help!" There was not a thing anyone could do about it. It was awful. Soon there was silence; we never heard or knew what happened to them. We just assumed that they went down in the water. The water was so cold that they wouldn't have been able to stand it for more than a few minutes.

CHAPTER 11

Landfall

We were cruising along pretty steadily now, the snow had stopped, and the weather was breaking up a little. I had no idea if we were close to being on course or not, but I guess Homer knew all along that we were OK. The closer we got to our destination, the more essential it was to maintain radio silence. We were not supposed to try to transmit on any frequency, or even talk to each other any more, because the Germans had intercepting stations all around and could, if they had heard us, pinpoint our location in no time at all.

About 6:00 a.m. our time, we began to see a little daylight, but, as we were above the clouds, we still could not see the water. Joe, my co-pilot, helped me an awful lot with the actual flying, as I was kept busy watching all of the instruments and checking everything to be sure we had no malfunctions. On the dash, we had a super-fantastic instrument, the exact name of which I've forgotten. It had a horizontal line which remained stationary. That horizontal line represented the horizon. Another line represented the wings. This marvelous instrument indicated if you were flying straight and level. If the line representing your wings rose above the stationary line, it indicated that you were climbing. If it appeared below the stationary line, it indicated that you were descending. If the line was higher at the right, it indicated that your right wing was too high, and if it angled below the line, the reading meant that the wing on that side was too low. It was the one instrument you depended on constantly, though sometimes you would have a tendency to disbelieve the reading. The indicator might say that you were flying level, but your body felt tilted to one side or the other. You had better believe the instrument.

Going on 7:00 a.m., we were getting increasingly anxious and worried about ever seeing land, any land, again. I was sweating out the gas gauges. I didn't know how much further we had to go. Then, at about 7:30 a.m., Homer, spotting something that looked like land, called me and said, "I think we made it."

"Homer, if you are right, I am going to kiss you," I said.

Soon he called again. "Turn to the right a little. I think I see our checkpoint."

I gradually reduced the altitude down to about 2000 feet, and we did pass our checkpoint, a town in Ireland. We knew then that we were close to Prestwick. Homer gave me the heading to fly, and I let the plane down a little lower. What time it was by their time, I don't know, but it was light and a little hazy. Although Prestwick was just a small place, it had a pretty good-sized airfield. Now we could see a lot of other planes in the air, and we knew that we were close.

Close to the field now, I called in for landing instructions. The girl in the tower who answered my call had such an accent that I couldn't understand her. I called a couple more times, and each time she rattled off some instructions so fast that I was still unable to understand. "Oh, nuts," I finally said. "I'm going to get in the traffic pattern and land behind one of the other planes." I followed one in, and we landed. As our wheels touched the ground, the guys actually cheered. It was a terrific feeling for all of us to be back down on land.

A couple of guys met us as we piled out of the plane. "Bring all of your personal luggage out of the plane," one of them said.

"What for?" I asked. "I thought I was taking this plane to England."

"No, sir," he said. "This is the end of the line for this plane. You will go the rest of the way by railroad. You will stay here overnight and leave tomorrow for your permanent base."

I couldn't believe it. "OK, pal," I said. "Just show me where I sleep." I was dead tired. So were the rest of the guys. None of us had slept a wink all night, and we were absolutely fatigued from all the tension and pressure we had been under.

No one asked me anything about the C-Rations or about what we were supposed to have transported with us. Nor did I say anything about them. We were taken to little Quonset huts with about 15 beds in each. I was so tired that I just plopped onto the bed in all of my flying clothes and boots. I fell asleep without even getting undressed or under the covers, and I slept straight through until the next morning. When I finally awoke the next morning, my body was itching terribly. While I was in Newfoundland, I had removed the tape that the doctor had wrapped around me in Nebraska. Now, I found myself all broken out in a rash. Sleeping in those hot clothes caused the rash to flare up and itch. Strangely enough, after I left Newfoundland and all the time I was in England flying in combat, I never once had any more stomach pain. For a long time, I attributed my relief to the change in climate. Years later, however, when I found out what was really wrong with me, I realized why the pains disappeared. After I returned home from service and had X-rays taken, I learned that I had an ulcer, and I was told by my doctor that ulcers usually flare up in the fall of the year.

CHAPTER 12

Dismal Christmas

The following day was December 24, Christmas Eve. We were put aboard a ferry, by which we crossed a large body of water. Whether it was a river, a lake, or what, I don't know; but we were on it practically all day. That night, we boarded a troop train, where we slept all night while the train just stood. The next day was Christmas. We traveled on that train all day long, with nothing to eat but some cans of hash and cold cans of beans. Our morale reached its lowest point that Christmas Day, 1943.

When we disembarked from that train the following day, we were hauled by trucks to our final destination in England. I was hoping that we would get stationed at a good base. During the war, there were hundreds of air bases in England, some of them just temporary installations, where living quarters were not very good — mostly all Quonset huts and restrooms situated in another building about a half block away. To shave and shower, you had to walk out of your hut and down to the bath house. At 4:00 a.m., when it's cold and damp, and you're half asleep, that's not much fun.

We struck it lucky; we were put in a permanent Air Force base, where we had nice brick buildings with separate rooms, inside washrooms, a large recreation hall with pool tables and ping-pong tables, and a large dining room. I understand that it had been formerly a training academy for British Air Force pilots — something like West Point. Right outside of Cambridge, England, home of the famous Cambridge University, the base was named Bassingbourn. When we were not flying, we went into Cambridge every weekend.

CHAPTER 13

War — First Glimpse

Upon arrival at our living quarters, we passed by the flight line, where the planes were coming back from a mission. We watched as the guys climbed out of the planes — all worn out, some injured, some dejected, all showing signs of the struggle they had just been through. In that moment, like a flash, I realized, *Man, this is war, and in just a few days, we are going to be doing the same thing.* A sick feeling passed over me.

How long it was before we started flying missions, I don't know exactly — possibly two or three weeks. I believe we had to have more trial runs and more training of some kind. When we did start flying, the first pilot of a crew, like myself, was required to fly co-pilot with some experienced crew for two missions. I flew as a co-pilot twice and then took my own crew from then on. As I have said, Bassingbourn was a very nice place; of all the military air bases in England, it was the best. They furnished us bicycles — or, rather, we bought them — to get from our barracks to the flight line. The distances between the building and the flight line and briefing room were too great to walk.

Joe Stoiber, my co-pilot, and I shared a room on the second floor, the first room in the hall next to the stairs. On the days we were scheduled to fly a mission, a man would come around and knock on our door at about 3:00 or 4:00 a.m. When he started up that flight of stairs, we heard every step he took. Seldom could we get to sleep the night before the day of a mission. When you were scheduled for a mission, your name would appear on the bulletin board the day before. But you wouldn't know your destination until the next morning at briefing. As soon as your name was posted, then the rumors would begin flying — usually started by the guys who were not going, with the intent of getting you all worked up or more scared than you already were. "Hey, I heard you guys are going to Russia tomorrow." Or, "Hey, you guys got a long one coming up. I heard it was going to be a 12-hour mission, with no fighter escort." And so forth. When we had a day off, we started our share of the same kinds of rumors.

CHAPTER 14

Preparing for Missions

The date of my first mission was January 29, 1944. The most anxious moment of the briefing was when they would uncover the large map on the wall, and you would see the line drawn across the map to the target of the day. If it was a long line, you would hear a big groan from all of the pilots in the room. All the pilots were briefed in one room, the navigators and bombardiers in another, and the gunners in still another.

We had ten 50-caliber machine guns on every plane. After the briefing, usually at 5:00 or 6:00 a.m., we'd all load up in trucks and be driven out to our ship. Once we were aboard, they would bring the bombs out and load them on. The bombs, some of which were huge, were carried on flatbed trailers. We usually carried ten 500-lb. bombs or five 1000-lb. bombs. The 1000-lb. bombs were about six or eight feet long and about eighteen inches in diameter. Each bomb was loaded into its own hangar. After the bombs were loaded, detonators were inserted somehow. Without a detonator, a bomb would not explode when it hit the ground. Detonators were sometimes defective, and bombs would hit the ground and just lie there without ever exploding. Detonators could also be set to cause a bomb to explode before it hit the ground so as to scatter shrapnel all over.

After loading and being all set to go, we sometimes had to sit and wait for an hour or sometimes two. Those were the nervous moments — waiting to take off. Delays were caused by several things, but mainly by weather conditions, often fog. It was always foggy in England in the morning, and we had to wait for the fog to lift a little. Sometimes we would wait for three hours, and then they would scrub the mission altogether. But that didn't happen very often.

They once scrubbed a mission after we had gotten up in the air and in formation. I was so glad that they did, because I had had a terrible feeling that I would never come back from that one. It was the kind of mission where everything seemed wrong. To begin with, it was on Easter Sunday, and it was a 10-hour job on, which we were supposed to be going to Posen, Poland. From the start, I didn't like anything about it. And I especially hated the idea of a bombing mission on Easter. I just knew I wasn't coming back. It was the one and only time I'd ever had that deep feeling. When we got the word to turn back for some technical reason, I was tickled to death. I felt like I'd received a new lease on life.

CHAPTER 15

Life at Bassingbourn

Except when we were flying a mission, it didn't seem as if we were fighting a war. Life at Bassingbourn was pleasant. We had comfortable living quarters. In fact, we were better off than most everybody who was fighting in any branch of the service. This was 100% better than sleeping in a foxhole or in the mud and rain, or tramping through the snow and eating meals out of cans. At least, at night we could come home and sleep in a nice, clean, warm bed and have a refreshing bath. Our recreation room was very large, and it was located on the main floor of the building we lived in. The sleeping rooms were on the second floor. In our recreation room, we had several pool and ping-pong tables, snooker tables, card tables, and a nice bar. Our dining room was also in the same building, and before going to bed, if you were hungry and wanted a snack, you could just go into the kitchen and get whatever you wanted.

Usually the cooks had sandwiches made and wrapped just for that purpose.

About the most uncomfortable thing we were required to do, when the air-raid sirens sounded in the middle of the night, was to jump out of bed and run outside and down into the air-raid shelter. That was very annoying. Just about the time you would get to sleep, that darned siren would sound. And you would be so tired. The German Air Force would come over occasionally and drop some bombs, and sometimes they were pretty close. Of course, our base and everything in England was completely blacked out at night, so it was hard for them to pinpoint their bombs. But, nevertheless, whenever the siren sounded, out we went, down into a concrete shelter below the ground. Sometimes we would just lie on the floor and sleep until the "all clear" was sounded. Some nights I was so tired, maybe after a mission, that I wouldn't even get out of bed. "Oh, the hell with it," I would say. "If God wants me to die tonight, I would just as soon die in bed."

England was full of air-raid shelters. Every town had them all over. If you were downtown shopping and the sirens sounded, there would be a mad rush for the shelters. When we went to Cambridge at night, of course, the town was blacked out. You couldn't see two feet in front of you. The only way that we could find the pubs or dance halls was to listen for the music. They didn't even want you to light a cigarette on the street at night. And if you lit a flashlight, they would almost throw you in jail.

In winter in England, it gets dark very early in the afternoon — about 4 o'clock — and stays dark until about 7:00 a.m. There was very little daylight in winter. However, in summer, it stays light until 11 o'clock at night, and daybreak comes very early in the morning. Inasmuch as I flew most of my missions in January, February, March, and April, we had much darkness. In May, toward the end of my stay there, we had a lot more daylight.

I visited London many times while I was in England. From where we were, London was about a 55-minute train ride away. London is a fantastic city, and very large. We watched the changing of the guard at Buckingham Palace and found that very interesting.

CHAPTER 16

Diary: Bombing Missions

We flew all of our missions and did all of our bombing prior to the Normandy Invasion. In fact, the purpose of our missions was to drive the Germans back further and further all the time. We flew 30 missions in all during the months of January, February, March, April, and May of 1943. I kept a diary in which I wrote about each of the missions after we had completed it and returned to the base. This is the diary that I kept during those months, with the destination of each mission, the length of time we were out, the events that took place, our results, and some of the thoughts I had at the time.

MISSION #1 Saturday, January 29, 1944
FRANKFURT

Today I went on my first mission over Germany. I rode co-pilot for Lt. Newquist, an old B-26 pilot, a good egg, and a fine pilot. We were up at 4:00 a.m. I didn't get back from town until 1:00 a.m., so at 4:00 a.m., I wasn't too eager to get out of the sack. Had breakfast and went to briefing at 5:00. Our target for today was the city of Frankfurt. We got all of our equipment together and were out to the ship at 0650. It was still very dark, and the gunners were already there getting their guns in. The ground crew was busy giving the ship the last-minute check. They had been up practically all night, getting the ship ready for the mission. Our bomb load was twelve 500-pound demolitions.

At 0725 everything was set, and we started engines. This was a maximum-effort job, and everything was being put into the sky except the colonel's jeep. At 0735 all the ships were taxiing in their respective order to the runway. The group leader was on the runway first, got the "go sign," and was off the ground right on the dot. We all followed suit in 30-second intervals. The formation-assembly altitude was 20,000 feet over the field, but when we got our altitude, no one was able to find the leader to get into formation. We got tired of flying in circles, so we went to the coast and tacked onto another formation, whom we hoped were going to the same target.

When we were about an hour from the target, the left oxygen system went dry. So half the crew had to use walk-around bottles. We didn't encounter any opposition until about a half hour from the target. Then the flak started bursting all around us, and we had a few fighter attacks. The flak over the target was pretty thick and accurate. We had a few close bursts, and we got a hole in the rudder about the size of a golf ball.

Somebody certainly wanted this town of Frankfurt to be blown to heck, because this was just about the largest force of U.S. heavies to hit any one target. There were more than 800 Forts on the raid. The sky was simply black with bombers, fighters, and smoke from flak. The bomb doors opened up on the Initial Point, and in a few minutes everybody's bombs were away. There was a solid undercast below, and we couldn't see the bombs hit, but they must have hit something because the smoke rose above the clouds.

The Luftwaffe had a busy day. We saw about 15 fighters, who made a few attacks after the target. I don't think they lasted long, because there were too many P-38s around. Two ME-110s had a little difficulty deciding who should get out of the other's way, but I guess they were a couple of stubborn Dutchmen, because they ran head-on into each other and exploded into a million pieces.

We saw one Fort get hit and go down, but he wasn't in our group.

The mission was 7 hours long.

MISSION #2 Sunday, January 30, 1944
BRUNSWICK

I made the team again today. I was riding co-pilot for Bob Fancher, an old classmate of mine. We had gone through flying school together and graduated together at Columbus, Mississippi, in May. His group left Kearney about a month before we did, came over on the boat, and had already had five missions when I got here. First pilots usually ride along as co-pilots on the first two or three raids to get the hang of things. We were briefed at 0530 this morning, and it was another long raid. The target was an aircraft factory at Brunswick, Germany. Three divisions with full strength were going in, with some of them hitting the town as well. Col. Putnam, our CO, was in the lead ship, so the 91st must have led the wing today.

We were off the ground at 8 o'clock sharp. We had a couple of pathfinders along. The formation assembled at 12,000 feet. Fancher was leading the second element of the composite squadron. At 10 o'clock, we were on course and climbing to altitude over the North Sea. When we reached the enemy coast, we were at 20,000 feet and kept climbing to bombing altitude, which was 25,000 feet. We were over enemy territory about an hour and fifty minutes before we reached the target.

The fighters started showing up about 45 minutes from the target. They are easy to spot by the single contrail. The trails look like a skywriting advertisement. The fighters will mill around a formation a while and look it over, staying out of range of our .50 cals. They definitely pick on straggling Forts that are lagging behind the formation. Then they all come down on him like a bunch of bees for the kill.

These German pilots are either terribly dumb or plenty brave, because their attacks are always head-on into a formation, doing a half-roll and barreling down toward the low group at about 500 mph. The low group ordinarily takes the beating. It seems to me that it would take a heck of a lot of guts to come screaming head-on into a formation of 80 to 100 Forts with everybody and their cousin blazing away at you with .50 cals. But they do it every day, so I guess they have plenty of guts. One thing I'm sure of, and that's the fact that the German pilots are good pilots. You can tell by the way they handle their planes. Maybe "Herr Boebbels" threatens his boys, so they have to come up and fight.

On the first fighter attack, they hit a Fort in the low group, and he went down smoking, and we saw three chutes come out before the ship exploded. An ME-109 came barreling through, carrying a bomb behind him on a long cable, and just missed our lead ship. The bomb exploded pretty close to the formation, but I don't think anyone was hit by it. We saw another Fort go down over the target, and I think he was on fire.

Our gunners knocked down a couple of Germans, and, once in a while, a kraut would come diving through us with a P-47 or P-38 on his tail. I feel sorry for them then, because they don't have a "Chinaman's chance" with a 47 on their tail.

We were over the target at 12 o'clock, dropped our load, and started for home. It sure is a grand feeling to get rid of those bombs. We were ducking in and out of high clouds around the target, which helped ward off a lot of fighter attacks. If it were clear up there, I think we would have caught heck because there were plenty of "kraut eaters" up there, trying to knock us down.

On the way home, we ran into a few flak areas, which were very inaccurate. We also had a few fighters, but our P-47 escorts gave us good cover. It's sure a wonderful sight to see a bunch of P-47s up there.

One of our boys came back on the deck with two engines out.

An engineer in one Fort had his leg blown off by a 20 mm shell. A radio operator in another ship got a piece of flak through the stomach and died on the way home. We were pretty lucky and didn't get a scratch.

✈ ✈

Front row left to right—Gail Garner, Ernest Ellington, John Anding, Robert Megchelson, Robert Hettinger, Norman Mansfield
Back left to right—Homer Glass, Louis LaHood, Joseph Stoiber, Mort Canter

MISSION #3 Thursday, February 3, 1944
WILHELMSHAVEN

Today I took my crew on their first raid. We raided the city of Wilhelmshaven. We had one of the oldest ships on the field, and we had a lot of trouble with superchargers. The mission was long and tiresome, and we had a tough time staying in formation, because two superchargers were not working all the way to the target. Then later on, a third one went bad. We bombed from 30,000 feet. We had very few fighter attacks and saw very little flak today, which was very unusual. But I was glad, because we had to drop out of formation, because we had a loss of power due to the loss of our superchargers. I burned up the only good engine I had trying to catch up to the formation.

On the way home, it sprung an oil leak, and oil was really pouring out of it; so, I had to feather it. So, we came home on three engines and never did catch the formation.

✷ ✷ ✷

MISSION #4 Friday, February 4, 1944
FRANKFURT

We went back and hit Frankfurt again today. Every time we go to Frankfurt, it's an all-out attack. Today, again, there were almost 1,000 Forts over the town. Our group was leading today, with Col. Alford in the #1 ship. We were blown way off of our course, or else the navigators had their heads up and locked, because we flew right over the Ruhr area, better known as "Happy Valley." It was the most heavily defended section in the whole country — as we found out, because they threw up everything at us except their canteen cups. And those boys down there are really checked out on those guns, because they had us sweating plenty. We had flak bursting right inside the formation all the time. Some bursts were black, some white, and some red. I don't think there was one plane that didn't come back full of holes. They got so close at times that I could hear the explosion and feel the concussion bounce the ship all around. That's too darned close for me!!

We got our bombs away over the town but couldn't see if we hit, because there was a solid undercast below.

We didn't see any fighters today. Maybe they had a day off, or maybe they saw all the P-47s, -38s, and -51s that were along with us.

On the way home, I'll be damned if they didn't fly us right back over the Ruhr again — of all the stupid things to do. I was flying in the #3 position on the left of the lead ship, flown by Col. Alford. And about right in the center of Happy Valley, he got hit in one of the inboard engines, and it started to smoke. He started down, and I followed him awhile until he disappeared into the clouds. The boys saw some chutes come out of the ship. That's the last we saw of him.

We joined another formation and came home. Our ship was all full of holes.

MISSION #5 Saturday, February 5, 1944
BURGESS

We had a comparatively easy raid today. We bombed an airfield in central France near Burgess. We went over at 15,000 feet, and the formation was excellent. We met no enemy opposition today and no flak at all.

When we were in the target area, an FW-190 took off and climbed up toward the formation only to meet a half-dozen P-38s on the way up, who drove him back into the ground on fire. There would be more fighters in the air if our fighter pilots would give them a chance to take off. But our fighters go down and get them as they are just taking off and hit them about halfway down the runway, and they don't have a chance. They also strafe the airfields continuously. They must destroy just as many on the ground as they do in the air. We hit the airfield beautifully right in the center of the hangar and administration section, and the smoke rose to 15,000 feet.

MISSION #6 Sunday, February 20, 1944
OSCHERSLEBEN

Today was a long haul to Oschersleben. We flew the low group and went in at 14,000 feet, which, at first, sounded like a suicide raid to us. Because the last time we went to Oschersleben, we lost 69 Forts, and now we were going in at 14,000 feet, which is too damned low to be flying over Germany. Those "Kraut Heads" can really pick you off with flak at that altitude. However, we were lucky and missed most of it.

We had pretty good cloud cover as well as fighter support. The target area was as clear as a bell. We could see the factories as plain as day. There was a lot of snow on the ground, and there didn't seem to be a living thing down there. Guess everybody was in their shelters, and I don't blame them.

All except the anti-aircraft batteries, and they were busy throwing things at us. But we went in, in spite of the flak barrages over the target, and hit the factories right on the button. We made a sharp turn off of the target, and I was able to look back and see the smoke. It was black as coal and rising high into the sky.

We had several fighter attacks on the way home. Our right waist gunner nicked an ME-410, who was shooting rockets at the formation. An FW-190 surprised us all when he came barreling through and almost went through our cockpit. He came by so fast nobody even got a shot at him. He went by us and hit Lt. Kidd's ship, who was flying right behind us. His ship went down smoking, and a few chutes were seen coming out.

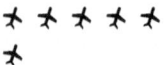

MISSION #7 Monday, February 21, 1944
OSNABRÜCK

We were supposed to bomb Osnabrück today. Major Berry was leading our group, and our group was flying high. Berry isn't the best leader in the Air Force and proved it several times today, as everything was pretty well screwed up. The formation was terrible on the way over, especially when we were climbing to altitude over the sea. However, we managed to stay in there somehow. We were off course all the way to the target, and, as a result, we caught a lot of flak. The weather wasn't too good, either. There was a solid undercast below, and we never saw the ground.

When we got to the target area, the leaders couldn't find the target, and the place was full of planes. So, they started a search, or so it looked to me. They made a 360-degree turn to the left. The bank was exceedingly steep, and, as a result, a lot of ships were left behind — naturally. That's when the fighters came in. They hit the boys behind us pretty hard, and I saw one Fort go down smoking.

We lost four ships right there. Among them were Spence Osterberg and his crew. I didn't see him go down, however, but I think I heard someone say that they saw them all bail out.

Well, we never did find the primary target and thought we were going to fly all over Germany carrying this load of bombs. I had Lassie that day, and we had supercharger trouble as usual and had a hell of a time staying with the formation. At one time I was indicating 190 mph trying to catch up. They finally picked a target of opportunity on the way out and bombed it. I think it was a German airfield. But I doubt that we hit it. I hate those screwed-up missions. Nobody knows what's going to happen next, and so many things can happen.

Well, we finally came back, and I was dead tired, trying to keep that airplane running and in formation. Every time I fly that ship, I swear to God I'll never fly it again. Guess the only way I'll get rid of it is to take it up to the graveyard and crash it.

When we got back over England, we had 90% cloud cover, and instead of making a procedure instrument letdown, the major found a hole and made a run for it. It's pretty tricky to bring an 18-ship formation down through a hole. Well, I guess he thought he could do it OK, so he dropped the nose and headed for it, and so did everyone else. I was way behind my leader, and I was indicating 210 mph and descending about 2500 feet per minute. I was expecting the wings to go flying off at any minute.

We all got through the hole all right, but the formation was broken all to the devil. I didn't bother trying to get back into formation, because I had just enough gas to make the field, and that's all. A couple of warning lights were on, so I just went in and landed. The mission was a GFU.

✈ ✈ ✈ ✈ ✈
✈ ✈

MISSION #8 Thursday, February 24, 1944
SCHWEINFURT

Today we went back and bombed the famous Schweinfurt ball-bearing works. They put every available plane in the air today. I didn't take Lassie today, because she was in the hangar, where she is most of the time.

This looked like it was going to be a tough raid, maybe because of the bad impression left there on the raids in August, when we took a terrific beating. In fact, our squadron was completely wiped out.

We didn't have too much trouble, although there was a heck of a lot of flak over the target. In fact, it was so thick we couldn't see the wings of the Forts ahead of us. They were throwing everything they had up at us. We were really doing some excessive evasive action. I was even doing a little individual evasive action. They were even shooting rockets up at us. They come up just like a skyrocket. You can spot them by the straight white streak of smoke they leave behind.

We hit the target well, though, and so did the wing that went in ahead of us. We could hardly see the target for the smoke left by the bombs of the ships ahead.

We had a few fighter attacks right in the target area. They were ME-110s, but I don't think they hit any ships in our Group. On the way in, I saw two Forts blow up in the air after they were hit by fighters. It's certainly a demoralizing sight to see a Fort blow up. It's indeed a terrific explosion, and if there are any ships close enough, the explosion will also get them.

We got back all right. I guess we had a few small flak holes in the ship. The mission was more than 7 hours long.

✈ ✈ ✈ ✈ ✈
✈ ✈ ✈

MISSION #9 Friday, February 25, 1944
AUGSBURG

It looks like we are going deeper into Germany every day. Today we were within a stone's throw of the Swiss Alps. The target for today was an aircraft factory at Augsburg. The Eighth Air Force is certainly going all out for the Luftwaffe. Guess they want to knock out the fighters before the invasion starts. I wish the darned invasion would start so that we can hurry and get this mess over with. This is getting darned old. And besides, I want to go home!!

This sure was a long ride, and I wasn't feeling well, anyway. We went in at 20,000 feet and came out at 15,000 feet.

We didn't hit any flak until the target, and then there wasn't too much. We had good fighter cover in and out. We also had a bunch of B-24s flying on our left, which is good cover, in the respect that when the Germans see Forts and Libs together, they go right for the Libs because they are easier to knock down, and there aren't so many guns firing at them.

I saw an ME-110 go through a formation ahead of us all alone and hit a Fort, and it started smoking and started down. I watched it all the way. I saw some chutes come out. The ship was really out of control. It did a couple of wingovers and then spiraled and spun on down to the ground. It seemed to take an hour for it to reach the ground. There were half a dozen fighters circling it all the way down; I couldn't tell if they were friendly or not. I finally saw it hit and explode. It was a terrific red explosion, and the smoke was black and rose very high. We were right about at the German border, and the boys who jumped might have landed in Holland or Belgium.

It seemed like it took hours before we got to Augsburg. We took off about 8 o'clock this morning, and I guess it was about 2:00 p.m. when we hit the target. We were carrying 42 incendiary bombs. When these incendiaries go out, they tumble like a bunch of beer bottles.

We were very close to Switzerland. It was kind of tempting to head for those Alps, land in a peaceful country, and sweat out the war. This is one time I was wishing a Jerry would come through and hit an engine or something; I certainly would have headed for the Alps.

We hit the factory and started home with comparatively no trouble, except that I got sick as the devil on the way home. It was such a long ride, and I think we were on oxygen for seven hours. I smoked a cigarette at 17,000 feet and got a sore throat. I think the mission was more than 8½ hours long.

MISSION #10 Monday, March 6, 1944
BERLIN

This is the one I've been expecting for some time.

They started out three days in a row for Berlin and each time had to turn back because of bad weather. The first day, the fighters got all the way to Berlin and didn't know that the bombers had turned back. The third day, everyone turned back except one small force of 26 Forts, who went in and dropped their bombs. The Germans shot almost half of them down. I suppose the rest of them ran out of gas on the way home.

Now we were going back to Berlin after a few incipient attempts to hit the city. Now Hitler had a chance to get all of his fighters and flak guns up to Berlin. They might as well have sent Adolph a telegram this morning and told him that we were coming. Everybody was going today. I guess the Eighth Air Force put up more than 800 bombers and more than 900 fighters.

We took off at 8:00 this morning. I was flying Queenie, as Fancher is on leave; besides, Lassie is still in the hangar. Col. Milton was leading our group, and our group was leading the whole Eighth Air Force into Berlin. Our target was a ball-bearing factory in the suburbs, and the 2nd and 3rd Divisions were hitting targets in and around the city.

We were flying at 21,000 feet, and everything was going great on the way in. We got a little bit of flak, only because we were off course. We were due at the target at 2:45. It was a long ride in there. When you're over enemy territory, the time seems to go slow as hell. You want to get the hell out of there. We were over enemy territory about six hours today.

We had good fighter support until we were over Berlin, and then, I guess, they were busy with individual dogfights.

It was about 30 minutes from the target when we started getting hit by everything the Luftwaffe had left. We saw a bunch of planes in front of us and flying a little higher. They were crossing from right to left, out of range, and they were hard to recognize. Then "we'd had it!" They peeled off and came in at us head on. There were about 35 or 40 of them on the first attack, and they came in all at once. I had looked away momentarily, and when I looked back, they were on top of us, and all were blazing away. I could see the flashes coming out of the wing guns. I called them out to the gunners, and they started firing away at them. I grabbed the wheel and started some evasive action and kept bouncing the ship all around so they couldn't get a good shot at us. It makes me nervous to see a fighter line up at us for a shot.

Joe and I were both on the controls. If he'd see one lining up, he'd dump the nose; then I'd see one and pull up. We stayed in a good formation, though, regardless of all the evasive action. On the first attack, they hit a ship who was flying opposite us in our squadron. He had an engine smoking and went down. That was Lt. Evertson, and he had a brand-new ship. We were right up in front, and they were trying to knock out the lead group in a desperate attempt to halt the raid on their capital. They came around again, but there were a few missing this time. I guess our gunners had knocked a few down. They peeled off again and came in; 20-mm shells were bursting all around us, and we started our evasive action again. Joe and I were really sweating. It wouldn't have been so bad if we could have fought back, but we had to keep right on thundering through, and your best life insurance is to stay in close formation. And we did exactly that!

The Germans repeated their attacks two or three more times, and we still didn't see any of our fighters. I don't know where they were off to. Anyway, we roared on around the city, heading for the factory. The clouds were broken, and we could see Berlin. It's pretty big. There was also a lot of flak over the city.

We got around to the target, but the bombardiers couldn't see because of the clouds. So, they flew on over a part of the city, dropped the load, and came out. I don't think the bombing results were too good. However, I guess we broke a few windows.

After we'd left, I looked back and saw the smoke and fires, and the sky was full of flak bursts and black smoke, white rocket trails, fighter planes smoking and spinning down, bombers going down and exploding, and parachutes floating down. It was just a tremendous air battle — something like you see in pictures.

Our fighter escort showed up again after we left the target, and we had very few attacks on the way home.

I guess the Germans had more than 600 fighters in the air to stop the attack. And they were really desperate, too. Today's raid made me realize that these Germans weren't beaten yet — not by a long shot. The official report was that the Germans lost about 200 planes and that we lost 63 bombers and 11 fighters. We lost six ships in our 18-ship Group alone.

Best we stay away from Berlin after this. They don't like to have their capital city bombed! And that's not the half of it: I don't like to go there!!

✈ ✈ ✈ ✈ ✈
✈ ✈ ✈ ✈ ✈

MISSION #11 Wednesday, March 8, 1944
BERLIN

Well, we went back and bombed Berlin again today. Only this time, it was a lot different from the first time.

I had one of the new pilots for a co-pilot, and I had to do most of the flying.

We went over at 25,000 feet. There must have been 700 or 800 Bombers over Berlin all at once. We didn't have any trouble at all; there was not much flak and very few fighters.

I think everybody hit the target, too. When we left, the city was just a mass of smoke and fire.

On the way home, I had a little trouble. I lost all the oil out of one outboard engine, and it wouldn't feather. I shut it off, and it just kept windmilling; at times, it would run away. I thought a couple of times the propeller was going to fly off. I also lost all of the electrical system, and we were without a radio. We dropped out of formation and couldn't catch up. Then about a dozen P-47s came along and escorted us all the way home.

The mission lasted 8 hours and 20 minutes.

✈ ✈ ✈ ✈ ✈
✈ ✈ ✈ ✈ ✈
✈

MISSION #12 Thursday, March 9, 1944
BERLIN

Berlin again! Guess Doolittle wants the place blown off of the map. But I wish he'd come along with us sometime, instead of sitting on his fanny and telling all the people that he'd bombed Tokyo, Rome, and now Berlin.

This Berlin haul is sure a long, tiresome ride. I never thought I'd get so tired of sitting down. It took us more than 5 hours to get to Berlin and only 3 hours to come back. I thought we'd never get to the target. I figured we'd passed it up and would end up in Russia. There were two layers of clouds. The first layer was solid and about 1,000 feet off the ground. The second layer was up at more than 20,000 feet, and we were above that, so, we had very good cloud cover.

I don't think one German fighter was able to get off the ground. We didn't see a single one all day.

We finally reached the target about 2:45, and we were supposed to be there at 1:15 p.m. Our primary target was an aircraft factory on the outskirts of Berlin, but they couldn't find it; so they hit the secondary target, which was the center of the industrial section of the city.

The flak over the city was so thick we could hardly see through it, but it was a little bit lower than we were. We turned and drove right over the city, straight through all the flak, and dumped our load. The sky again was black with Forts over the city. They just came over in waves, dropped their loads, and kept right on going. I think Berlin took a terrific pounding today, because everybody was carrying even bigger loads than yesterday.

We dropped down to 15,000 feet on the way home. We drove right through a flak area, and our squadron got hit a little. My ship took a couple of direct hits. One hit right behind the tail gunner, and he's still shaking. It blew out the tail wheel. We had a piece knocked out of the elevators, a hole in each wing, and one shell burst right in front of my windshield. A piece hit the glass and cracked it, and I jumped four feet. If it hadn't been for the bulletproof glass, I'd be sporting a set of "store boughten" teeth.

This was the third raid to Berlin in four days. I was so damned tired that I couldn't fly formation more than 15 minutes at a time. I thought my arms were going to fall off a couple of times. This was a great day for the Eighth Air Force.

Losses: 7 Bombers, 1 Fighter

✈ ✈ ✈ ✈ ✈
✈ ✈ ✈ ✈ ✈
✈ ✈

MISSION #13 Saturday, March 18, 1944
OBERPFAFFENHOFEN

Well, this was that big-jinx mission. Everyone sweats out old number 13. I sweated it for about nine days, only to find it rather easy. We raided an airfield way down near Switzerland. The name of the place is a real tongue twister — "Oberpfaffenhofen." I can't pronounce it. It's all I can do to spell it. The trip was about 1,350 miles and one of the longest I've ever been on.

I flew the number 3 position in the low squadron of the composite group. We took off at 9 o'clock this morning. We rode and rode, and I thought we'd never reach the darned target. Finally got there about 3 o'clock. We saw very little flak, and what we did see was very inaccurate. We had very good fighter support from P-47s, P-51s, and P-38s.

However, a few ME-109s sneaked in for an attack in the target area. Our P-38 escort peeled off and jumped a bunch of Germans below us. Right after they left, I spotted about 8 ME-109s queued up for the kill from head on. I called them out to my gunners, and they started blasting away at them. The fighters came right in at us in the high group. I took some good evasive action so they couldn't get me in their sights. They were really peppering 20 mm at us, but we got by without a hit — thank the Lord! That's the last time they bothered us. I guess the American fighters got on them.

We dropped our loads on the target and headed for home. We were right on the edge of the beautiful Swiss Alps — and they certainly looked inviting. Every time we go close to those Alps, we lose a few planes. Today they reported that 16 American bombers landed there. The lucky boys. They can lie on their fannies in a nice, peaceful country, wait until the war is over, learn how to ski and skate, latch onto a little Swiss gal, and really enjoy life.

I thought we'd never get to that darned French coast on the way home. Finally made it, though, two hours later.

The mission was 9 hours long.

✈ ✈ ✈ ✈ ✈
✈ ✈ ✈ ✈ ✈
✈ ✈ ✈

MISSION #14 Monday, March 20, 1944
FRANKFURT

We went back to Frankfurt today, and most of us were rather pleased, because it is a little shorter than the usual runs lately. Not a lot, though. The trip is 1,000 miles.

Frankfurt has always been a tough target. I think this is my third trip there. They throw up a lot of flak and also have quite a few fighters in that area.

We took off at 8:30 this morning, and the assembly was lousy because there were a lot of high clouds. In fact, the whole mission was screwed up, due to a high overcast.

We flew the low group today. I was in the number 3 position in the first element. We got pretty close to Frankfurt and ran into this high cloud bank, and the whole wing got lost. Everyone was flying around in circles, it seemed.

It would have been a field day for Hitler if he had sent his fighters up, because we were spread out all over.

I don't think anyone hit the target. Our group dropped our bombs at random. We flew through some pretty accurate flak, and we got a few holes in the wings. The wing leader got tired of flying around Germany, so he called and told us to head back for England. So, everybody turned back. Our group got back together when we broke out into the clear somewhere in France.

I logged 7 hours on the trip.

✈ ✈ ✈ ✈ ✈
✈ ✈ ✈ ✈ ✈
✈ ✈ ✈ ✈

MISSION #15 Wednesday, March 22, 1944
BERLIN

I was afraid that this was going to happen, because we had a dance and party here at the base last night, and everyone was loaded — including myself. I got into bed at 2:00 a.m., and the alert officer came around and woke me at 3:15 a.m.

I knew then that it was going to be a long one, because they got us up so early. I rolled out of bed half asleep and still about two-thirds drunk. Boy, did I feel bad! I had breakfast, went down to briefing, and damned near fell flat on my face when I saw the target for the day was Berlin. I was flying 673B, and my position in the formation was the same as usual, number 3 in the first element.

This trip is always a back-breaker. It seems like it takes all day to get there and twice as long to get home. We drove and drove and finally reached the city at about 2:30 p.m. It was hardly worthwhile for me, as I was carrying the propaganda today. I had 3,000 pounds of leaflets in the bomb bay instead of TNT. I don't know what they said, because they were printed in German. They usually contain a bunch of propaganda telling the German people how strong the American Air Force is and stating facts about the Luftwaffe's losses, and that Germany and her people could be saved if they would overthrow their Nazi leaders, etc. Wish they'd hurry and do something and get this darned war over with.

We drove right smack over the center of Berlin. They were sending flak in barrages. The sky was covered with flak bursts, and we plowed right through it. We dropped our bombs right in the heart of town and blew up everything. Some of the planes carried incendiaries, and when we left the city, there were a thousand fires started. Black smoke was beginning to rise high into the sky.

We didn't see very many German fighters. However, other groups were hit pretty hard by the Luftwaffe. We got back to England without any trouble.

It's always a long drive back home. It's a great feeling to cross the French coast and head across the channel. I don't waste any time tearing off my oxygen mask and flak suit. They drive me nuts!

✈ ✈ ✈ ✈ ✈
✈ ✈ ✈ ✈ ✈
✈ ✈ ✈ ✈ ✈

MISSION #16 Thursday, March 23, 1944
MUNSTER

Our target today was an aircraft factory at Munster, Germany. We were up very early this morning and took off in the dark. The weather was really bad. The ceiling was about 400 feet, but we climbed up through and broke into the clear at about 5,000 feet.

It seems like we always fly in bad weather. Of course, the weather is always bad here, anyway.

This mission was all messed up, as usual. We went over at 20,000 feet. I was flying up in the high composite squadron. When we got to the target, the weather was closed in, so we had to use the pathfinder. The leaders made a couple of 360-degree turns right over the target and then lost it; we finally spotted a peaceful little town and blasted it right off of the map. All the while we were circling up there, the flak batteries were having a field day, throwing up everything they had.

We were lucky enough not to be hit by fighters, although the groups behind us were hit. The tail gunner saw a Fort get hit by a German; one wing fell off, and it started to spin. Then the other wing fell off. I don't think we lost a ship out of our group.

✈ ✈ ✈ ✈ ✈
✈ ✈ ✈ ✈ ✈
✈ ✈ ✈ ✈ ✈
✈

MISSION Friday, March 24, 1944
Schweinfurt (Abortive)

This was one hell of a day. I thought we'd had it! We took off at 8:00 a.m., assembled at 19,000 feet, and headed out over the North Sea. I was flying our new ship 673. We got halfway across Belgium, and our #2 engine started to throw oil. At first, it wasn't very bad. I kept a close watch on it for about five minutes. Then, all of a sudden, everything inside of it went to hell. I don't know exactly what caused it all. It was just internal failure. Oil flew in all directions. I hit the feathering switch immediately, but it was too late. The oil was all gone, and it was impossible to feather it. I said to myself, "Well, here we go again."

The prop kept windmilling and vibrating terribly, and, at times, it would over-speed and darn near shake the plane apart. I left the formation and turned back for England. We had some thirty minutes to go before we hit the coast. I kept fighting the engine and trying to slow it up. We had five 1,000-pound bombs aboard and had to wait until we got out over the water before we could drop them. We are not supposed to drop bombs at random in occupied countries. We reached the Channel about 30 minutes later and dropped them, and that helped a little. It made the ship lighter and a lot easier to hold altitude. I transferred all of the gas out of the #2 tank and shut off the fuel supply because I was afraid it would start burning.

The crew were all getting worried, because the plane was shaking so much. In fact, a couple of the boys were going to bail out over Belgium. They were all in the radio room, and I went back and told them not to worry; I thought it would be OK.

It took us about 40 minutes to cross the English Channel. There was an undercast, so we couldn't see the ground. The engine was getting hotter all the time, and pistons and rods were breaking into little pieces and flying out all over. Finally, the navigator figured we had reached England, so I started letting down to get below the clouds. Just then, the engine became red hot; sparks started coming out all over, and the prop started going faster and faster. I called the crew and told them that the engine was getting worse and that, in case it started to burn, I would give the signal for them to bail out.

Lou's plane Black Magic, upon returning from aborted mission to Schweinfurt, March 24, 1944. Picture taken by Ray Ward, fellow B-17 pilot, who had finished his tour of duty two days prior. Lou is at far right, bending over.

Just then, it started burning; there was oil all over the cowling, and it started. So I told the crew to get out because it might blow up. Glass didn't waste any time; he put his chute on and jumped out of the nose hatch. The boys in the back did some fast moving. Kunst, the waist gunner, kicked the door out; he stepped back and said to the tail gunner, "After you." And the tail gunner said, "Nothing doing, buddy. You go first." So, Kunst went out first, and three more followed him.

Before the rest of the boys had a chance to get out, the engine started to fall apart, and then the prop flew off. And I was glad to see it go. After it fell off, the fire stopped, and the plane stopped vibrating. So, the rest of the boys stayed in the ship. Joe and I weren't going to jump, anyway. No matter how bad the ship is shot up, if it's still running, I figure that I can fly it down and crash land.

We were about 40 minutes from our field, so we flew back on three engines. Got back and came in for a landing, and everyone was watching with their mouths wide open.

Glass sprained his ankle when he hit the ground, but the rest of the boys got down OK. Kunst landed in a tree. They all got back the following day.

PEORIA PILOT RUES DAMAGE TO 'BLACK MAGIC'—First Lt. Louis La Hood, 500 Loucks ave., Peoria, pilot of the Flying Fortress "Black Magic," looks ruefully at one of his four engines that lost its prop returning from a bombing raid over Germany. Lieutenant La Hood flew the ship back to its home base and landed without further damage. (Released by War Department.)

Newspaper photo of Schweinfurt mission.
Peoria Journal Star

MISSION #17 Tuesday, March 28, 1944
REIMS, FRANCE

This looked like a nice, short, easy raid to France. We hit an airfield at Reims. We bombed from 22,000 feet. Everything was OK on the way in; we got to the target, dropped our load, and blew the field all to heck. On the way back, we got hit by flak. We took a direct hit in the hydraulic system, and the fluid leaked out all over the ship. Well, that left us without any brakes. We had a hole as big as a basketball in the nose, right beside the navigator. I guess almost everybody in our squadron got hit.

We came back to the base and came in for a landing. Joe and I both figured we'd end up in the cornfield, because the brakes were out. But, luckily, we landed on the long runway. I came in short, and Joe cut the inboard engines before we hit the ground; he was on the hand pump, but it didn't work, either.

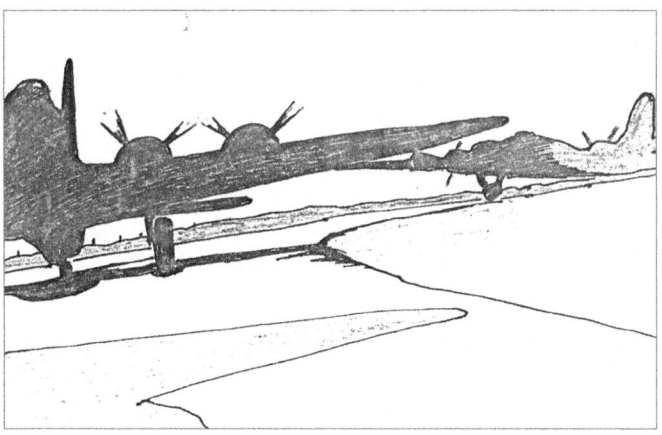

Joe is about the best co-pilot in the whole group. I can sure depend on that kid. He's always on the ball.

Well, anyway, by the time I got to the end of the runway, we had slowed up enough to turn off onto the grass, and I left it there.

Combat is rough!!

✈ ✈ ✈ ✈ ✈
✈ ✈ ✈ ✈ ✈
✈ ✈ ✈ ✈ ✈
✈ ✈

MISSION #18 Wednesday, March 29, 1944

BRUNSWICK

Today, we were supposed to hit a chemical and rubber plant at Brunswick, Germany.

I was leading the third element in the composite squadron, which is the toughest flight of all to lead. However, I held it in there fairly well. We assembled at 22,000 feet and climbed to 25,000 over the sea.

James and Downing were on my wings. When we got to the target, the weather was closed in; so we did pathfinder bombing over the city instead of the primary target. The flak was very heavy over the city, and we drove right through it. My right wingman, Downing, was shot down or else lost two engines and went down. Nobody seemed to see him get it. He didn't come back, so he must have had it. The left wingman was hit by flak over the target, and he lost two engines; but he kept right on coming. He made it home.

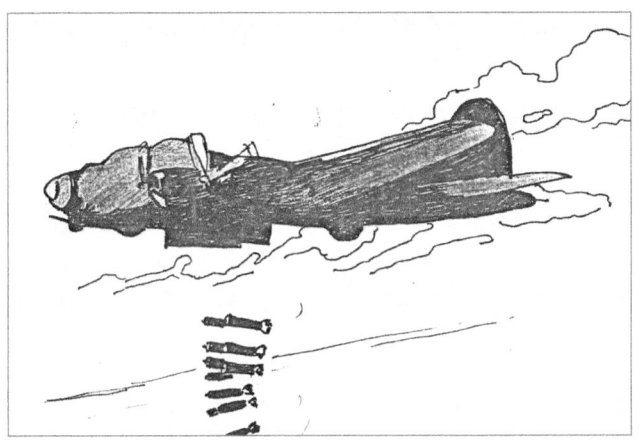

We saw scads of German fighters today. They knocked down a few Forts out of the Group on our left. Our P-51s were really battling it out with the Germans today. I witnessed two beautiful dogfights by a P-51 and a German, and I think each time, the P-51 emerged victoriously. They don't last long when a P-51 or P-47 gets on their tail. They try desperately to maneuver them off of their tail, but in a few seconds, it's all over. They start smoking, and down they go, spinning like a top.

When we got back to England, the weather was really bad. The clouds were practically on the ground. The whole formation got split up when we hit the clouds. I started down at 13,500 feet and didn't break out into the clear until 300 feet above the ground. I sure sweated that out!

Everybody was trying to land at once. The control officer was tearing his hair out.

✈ ✈ ✈ ✈ ✈
✈ ✈ ✈ ✈ ✈
✈ ✈ ✈ ✈ ✈
✈ ✈ ✈

SOME THOUGHTS WHILE FLYING MISSIONS

About 4:00 o'clock each afternoon, everyone is eagerly awaiting the notice to be posted on the bulletin board to see who will be flying on the mission for tomorrow. If your name appears there, the anxiety begins. Your stomach reacts with a little empty feeling. The thought never leaves you. You return to your room, try to relax, read a book, listen to music, finally go to bed, try to sleep, lay awake for a couple of hours, say many prayers.

Finally, you fall asleep, only to hear in a short time, the footsteps of the alert officer coming to awaken you. The knock on the door is a sickening sound. You get up, still in a drowsy stupor, and fumble around in the dark for your clothes. Oh, how I wish I was home!

You wash and shave and dress and go down to breakfast. It's still only 4:00 a.m. It's quiet at breakfast. Nobody talks much. You walk over and look at the big pan full of powdered eggs scrambled. Your stomach turns some more. You force down some food, because you know it will be a long time before you see any more. You finish eating and walk out into the damp, foggy morning air, get on your bike, and proceed to the flight line and briefing room — about a half-mile distance from the living quarters. Still very dark and damp and cold.

You can hardly wait to see the map and the target for today. You arrive and take a seat with all the rest of the pilots. In a little while, the commanding officer gets up, unveils the large map on the wall, and says, "Gentlemen, your target for today is…" If the line is long, you hear everyone in the room groan.

All of the information is given: target, altitude, point of assembly, each one's position in the formation, secondary target, etc., etc. After completing the briefing, we pick up our parachutes, flak suits, maps, and anything else you can think of. Oh, yes, chocolate candy bars — for energy — and an escape kit for each man, whose contents include maps of Germany, maps of France, some German and French money, some identification papers and pictures of you in civilian clothes, and some other items for your survival in case you should get shot down over enemy territory.

Ready to go now, we climb into trucks to be driven out to our plane, which is another half mile out on the field. By this time, the bomb crews have just finished loading the bombs on the plane. We usually carry ten 500-pound bombs or five 1000-pound bombs, depending on the target to be bombed. In the plane now, everyone is attending to their own specific duties: gunners checking their guns and ammunition; radio man checking receivers and transmitters; pilot and co-pilot going over checklist, checking all instruments, electrical system, hydraulic system, oil pressure, fuel, oxygen, etc. Usually your plane is in good shape for a mission because you have a maintenance crew for each plane. These guys take a lot of pride in their work. They stay up all night sometimes to get their plane ready for a mission. And when you come back from a mission, they are out there on the runway waiting to see how their plane is.

Now that everything is ready to go, you have only to wait for the signal to start engines. It's coming up on 7:00 a.m. and just beginning to get light out. You wait. The ceiling is usually very low in England in the early morning; it's foggy every day. You wait for the fog to lift a little. There are days when it is clear, and you can take off right away — but very seldom, at least at this time of year.

Finally, you get the signal to start engines. Sometimes, it's a major project to start an engine. You have to prime the engine with a hand pump in the cockpit; on the ground, they attach a booster battery to turn it faster. When engines start running, you must let them warm up sufficiently before taking off. The leader starts taxiing to the runway, and everyone follows in turn.

On a normal mission, there will be three squadrons of six planes each, a total of 18 bombers, unless it's a maximum effort. Then they might send four squadrons. So, there are 18 planes taxiing in a line to the runway. A fascinating sight. When the leader approaches the runway to be used, he stops, sets his brakes to hold the plane, and then races all four engines for a minute to clear the carburetors of excess gas so as not to have the engine choke out on takeoff.

He then turns and lines up the plane on the runway, watching for his signal from the flagman standing on the side of the runway. When the flagman drops the flag, the leader gives it all four throttles — feeding them slowly — and begins to roll down the runway, increasing the throttles as he goes. He watches the speed increase, being mindful that his plane is carrying a maximum load — between 50,000 and 60,000 pounds. With a big load, he has to get it up to 120 mph before he can get off. The runways are 5,000 feet long, and by the time he nears the end, he should have enough speed. He pulls back on the wheel steadily, still with full power. He's off, but he can't see; he's in the fog. He continues to climb straight ahead, using instruments, until he breaks into the clear.

In the meantime, 30 seconds have elapsed; the second plane gets the flag and rolls down the runway, and all the rest follow suit. When you get off the ground and are in the fog, you do not fly around in circles because you are liable to run into another plane. You must fly and climb straight ahead until you break out into the clear. Then you climb to the prescribed altitude to assemble your formation. It's usually 19,000 or 20,000 feet. The leader is up there first, and he is circling the area above our field. The second plane reaches altitude next, spots the leader, and flies over and assumes his position on the leader's wing. Then the third and fourth, until the entire 18-ship group is in formation. Then the leader proceeds to his "Initial Point" on the coast of England. In the meantime, other 18-ship groups have assembled. There might be six other groups at this altitude, gradually tacking onto each other as they head for the Channel.

Three Divisions — the First, Second, and Third — make up the Eighth Air Force, each with a different insignia on the tail. Ours, the First Division, has a triangle; another division has a square, etc. So, when these groups assemble with other groups, they assemble with groups with the same insignia. By the time you get to the Channel, you might have 100 planes in this formation. Then here comes another wing from the Second Division with another 100 planes, and another with 100 more planes, and they all proceed relatively close together. Each 18-ship group tries to keep their formation as tight as possible to ensure their own safety against enemy fighter attacks.

On each bomber, there are ten machine guns; so if a fighter attacks an 18-ship group, he has 180 machine guns shooting at him. Of course, they are not all in a position to shoot. However, most of them are. One of the major hazards about all of this firepower is the fact that, many times, our gunners accidentally hit our own bombers while shooting at enemy fighters. It's sometimes unavoidable.

Now that the three wings of 100 planes each have met, they proceed across the English Channel and head for their respective targets. This assembly is not done by accident. This is all predetermined at Strategic Air Command, Eighth Air Force Headquarters.

The flight across the Channel is almost monotonous. The continuous drone of the engines, plus the bright sun glaring through the cockpit windows, almost makes you feel drowsy, especially because you did not get much sleep the night before.

It is hard for me to describe the magnificent sight when a hundred planes are flying in formation above a solid blanket of white clouds with the sun shining so brightly and each plane leaving four contrails in the sky. It's unbelievable.

Crossing the Channel is a quiet time in the plane. No one is talking. It's a time to think. Everyone is left with his own thoughts. You wonder what is in store for you today. You wonder whether you will get back in one piece. The memory of your last mission lingers in your mind… all of those puffs of anti-aircraft shells exploding close to your plane, and how you escaped without having a piece of shrapnel rip into your body. Will this be the day? Sometimes your mind drifts into negative thoughts: We're on a futile mission…. Maybe my number will be up soon. You realize you can't allow yourself to think that way. You have to have faith — faith in God and faith in yourself. Prayer is the only answer. Prayer will give you the faith. It's the only thing that has kept you from becoming a nervous wreck.

Many times, when going across the Channel into Germany, I'd look out, see all those planes, and wonder silently: *What am I doing here? How did I get here? Whatever possessed me to choose this particular branch of the Service? Why am I up here getting shot at, when I know there are thousands of guys back home working in factories? Why wasn't I smart enough to get a job in a defense plant or something?*

Then, my thoughts would answer: *Well, maybe it's not so bad. There are a lot of guys worse off than me. Think of those poor guys on the islands in the South Pacific, fighting in those jungles and sleeping in foxholes in the rain and mud. No thanks! I'll take this.* I guess thinking about jungles and foxholes and mud and rain and Japanese snipers in trees is sort of a pacification. You don't feel so bad then.

Another matter that often occupies my thoughts as we make this crossing concerns my own qualifications for being the commander of this bomber, with nine guys aboard who look to me for dependability, have faith in me, and trust my ability for their safety and for their lives. I was not sure whether I could handle all of that responsibility. They would come to me with their problems, sometimes personal problems. How could I advise them, when there were problems that I couldn't solve for myself? I could not let them know or even suspect that I was unsure of a decision. I could not allow them to lose faith or confidence in me. No matter how scared I was at times, I could not let them know it.

I would think, *What qualifies me to sit in this seat, when just a couple of years before I was just a floundering 21-year-old, who had no idea where his life was going?* You decide you have to quit thinking these kinds of thoughts and take charge of the situation at hand, as these planes are crossing the Channel and slowly approaching enemy territory. They are slowly climbing to their prescribed bombing altitude, which is usually 30,000 feet. Of course, we have long since been on oxygen.

You put your oxygen mask on after 10,000 feet. You couldn't live very long without it above 15,000 feet. I remember that, while in training, they wanted us to realize the effects of being in altitude without oxygen. So, they put you and several others in a pressure chamber without oxygen. It takes only about 4 or 5 minutes, and then you pass out. Then they turn on the oxygen and revive you. They did that only once, and that was enough! With your oxygen mask on, you could still communicate on the intercom with your throat mike on.

As the planes are climbing to a higher altitude, the outside temperature is dropping below zero. It is not uncommon for the temperature to be 50 degrees below zero at 30,000 feet. Consequently, the machine guns on the plane have to be fired every so often to ensure that they don't freeze up, so that they will be operable when needed.

As I have mentioned before, this time of the flight is very quiet and tense. There is not much talking. Normal procedure calls for the gunners to alert the whole crew when they are going to test their guns, so that we can expect it and not be scared out of our wits. But, invariably, my top turret gunner would never say a word that he was going to test guns, and his guns were right above the cockpit, not two feet above our heads. Without a word of warning, he would let go with a blast out of his two machine guns, and Joe and I would jump 3 feet out of our seats. I swear, I almost had a heart attack many times.

He would stand right behind and between the pilot and co-pilot seat. So, when he would do that, I would get so mad at him that I would grab something and hit him on the shins, as he was standing on a platform, and all you could see was his legs.

Another thing that can scare the life out of you is when a squadron of six planes are in formation, with the leading three planes a little higher than the other three. When the tail gunner of the plane in front and above you test-fires his guns, the empty shell casings are ejected from his guns and fall and hit your windshield. Don't think that doesn't shake you up!

So many things about this war just don't make sense. As you fly over England, you see hundreds of thousands of American-made army vehicles — trucks, tanks, jeeps, guns, airplanes by the thousands. All kinds of planes, bombers, fighters — all brand new — waiting to be used. You don't have to be a mathematician or an economist to realize the hundreds of billions of dollars going down the drain. Why are we doing it? And you wonder, too, why all of these planes are going to Germany full of bombs to destroy a country that it took hundreds of years to build.

From the air, Germany is a very pretty country. The fields are sectioned off by hedgerows. There must have been many ancient structures and much history there. The Air Force could level a town in a matter of minutes. I felt very sorry for the German people. The Eighth Air Force heavy bombers would go over in the morning, and when they were returning, the medium bombers were going over. They would return early in the evening, and then the British heavy bombers would go over at night. So, they were being bombed around the clock.

I saw a picture of the town of Frankfurt, Germany. Every building in the town was flattened, except one. A church steeple stood high above all the rubble. The caption on the picture said, "God would not allow it."

When our leaders reach 30,000 feet, they level off and proceed to the target. To make the bomb run, they first have to locate their IP (Initial Point), from which they take a certain compass heading and make their bomb run. This is all previously calculated. Every plane is equipped with a Norden bombsight, but only the leader uses his, so that when the lead plane opens its bomb-bay doors and drops his bombs, all the other planes do likewise simultaneously. This is the most crucial time of the mission.

During the bomb run, you have to maintain a constant air speed and not bounce around too much. If you are in the middle of an enemy fighter attack or heavy anti-aircraft fire, you just have to fly right through it; there is nothing else you can do. This is where a big percentage of the bombers get shot down. It is a big relief to get rid of the bombs and get out of the area.

After dropping that load of bombs, the plane has lightened considerably, and the air speed increases. The leaders increase their speed, too, in order to get out of the area as quickly as possible. The planes in the rear of the formation now are having a hard time trying to stay close. You have to kick up your air speed in order to catch up. You try desperately not to be a straggler, because these are the ones that the German fighters pick on.

Flying back to England from a mission in Germany seems to take forever. It usually takes 2 to 3 hours, depending on how far in you went. You are tired and still sweating out the anti-aircraft bursts. Your oxygen mask is driving you nuts; you've had it on now for about 5 hours and can't wait to yank it off. Finally, when you are about halfway through France, they begin to let down to below 15,000 feet, and then off comes the oxygen mask. What a relief! By this time, everyone is starved, so they begin to grab for the candy bars.

Now you are approaching the English Channel once again. This time, you are glad to see it, because now you know that you are fairly safe and that it won't be long before you are home again. Now you yank off the flak suits. They are heavy. A flak suit is like a bulletproof vest, only it's a slipover, without sleeves. You slip it over your head and it protects your front and back down to your waist. It looks like a baseball catcher's chest protector, except that the inside is heavy-gauge steel.

Coming home is a happy time, with a lot of laughing and kidding around and talking about the mission — things you saw, fighters you shot at, planes you saw go down, who they were, and if they bailed out, etc. Now, at last, you are over the mainland, and all of the groups separate from the formation and return to their respective fields. Our 18-ship group continues on to our field. When we arrive at the Base, our altitude is about 1500 feet. Then the leader goes first. He peels off in a real steep bank and drops into the traffic pattern for landing. Then the rest of the planes follow, each one peeling off in turn. It is a fascinating sight to see all of these bombers peeling off one after the other.

You come in for a landing. If you set it down nice and smooth, the crew claps and cheers. If you bounce a couple of times, they give you the raspberries. After flying formation for 6 or 7 hours, just staring at your wingman, your depth perception plays tricks on you. So when you come in for a landing, suddenly you're looking at the runway, and sometimes you just don't make a perfectly smooth landing. Who cares! As long as you're on the ground — that's the important thing! After a long mission, your forearms are so sore and tired. They feel like they are all cramped up from gripping the wheel so tightly all day. Your hind end feels like two boils. You sit on your parachute straps, and they practically cut into your flesh. The pilot's seat is all metal — no padding or cushions.

You roll to the end of the runway and stop; then you taxi over to our parking area. Everybody piles out except me. I like to shut off the engines and just sit there for a few minutes. Mostly I'm too tired and drained to move, but mostly to just enjoy the silence. For 7 or 8 hours, you've heard nothing but the roar of those four engines. And now, oh! How great the silence is.

Now the maintenance crew is coming into the plane to check it all over, asking if there are any major problems, checking to see how much damage was done, etc. I finally climb out, and we all load up in the truck again and head for the interrogation room. You enter the room, and the noise begins again. There must be 150 guys in the room, all talking at once, laughing and yelling, and gulping down the refreshments. I can't wait to get out of there, get back to my quiet room, and flop on the bunk.

We leave and head for our building. It's now about 3:30 p.m. I feel like I can sleep for 24 hours. Somebody says, "Hey, the bulletin board."

"Oh, my God! Go check the bulletin and see if we are on for tomorrow."

MISSION #19 Saturday, April 8, 1944
OLDENBURG

We hit an airfield at Oldenburg today. It was a fairly good raid. We went over at 22,000 feet, and the weather was very clear — that is, of course, after we finally got off of the ground. A heavy ground fog delayed takeoff for a couple of hours, as usual.

We went in at 20,000 feet and were carrying a maximum load of 500-pound demolitions. There weren't any enemy fighters around that I could see. However, the flak was intense. The more I see of that darn flak, the more I hate it! I sure sweat that stuff out lately.

The target area was very clear, and the airfield came up beautifully. The bombs hit the end hangar and walked right up through a bunch of workshops and buildings.

On the way home, we were continuously flying through flak barrages. We got by without any serious damage. Had several small flak holes in the wings and fuselage.

✈ ✈ ✈ ✈ ✈
✈ ✈ ✈ ✈ ✈
✈ ✈ ✈ ✈ ✈
✈ ✈ ✈ ✈

MISSION #20 Thursday, April 13, 1944
SCHWEINFURT

This is one place I hate to go to. This is my second trip to Schweinfurt. There are an awful lot of German fighters around that area, and it seems like every time the force goes there, they get the hell knocked out of them.

I led the second flight in the composite squadron, and our altitude was about 25,000 feet. Lassie has a heck of a time getting up that high. We usually burn up half of our gas getting up to altitude and assembling; then we go easy on it on the way home and hope and pray that we have enough to make it.

I started out flying from the co-pilot's seat today, because that is the only place one can see to fly that position. But I didn't do so well, so I changed back to the left seat and had to stretch my neck to see. We hit a little flak on the way in. Our fighter support was good until about a half hour before we reached the target. Then I guess they were too busy with the Germans. And there were plenty of them!

I spotted a flock of planes ahead of us. They seemed to be just milling around. I can always tell the Germans by the way they fly. They just drive around in bunches — like buzzards. They'll size you up and plan an attack. If the formation looks loose and vulnerable in spots, they'll come in and rake it every time, without fail! These fighters were too far away to distinguish, so the boys kept tracking them. I guess they looked us over and saw that our formation was pretty tight, so they decided to hit the outfits on both sides of us.

There must have been a hundred of them, and they peeled off and headed in with their wing guns blazing and the 20 mm flashing. I saw three of them go down before they reached the bombers. The first time they raked the formation, they knocked out six Forts. I saw two ships burst into flames simultaneously. Another got the controls shot up, did a perfect loop, and then went straight down. Two others blew up a little way away from the formation. There were parachutes all over the sky. The Germans made a big circle, came back through again, and shot down a few more, but our gunners were getting some of them, too.

Then they hit the outfit on our left. On their first pass, they got two Forts; one went down with a couple of engines smoking, and the other burned awhile and then blew up. All this time, I'm watching them and sweating and praying that they don't hit us next. Finally, the P-51s showed up, and then there was a nice, big battle.

We went on and hit the target well. The flak over the target was thick. We hit the ball-bearing factories for the fourth time — and I hope it's the last!

✈ ✈ ✈ ✈ ✈
✈ ✈ ✈ ✈ ✈
✈ ✈ ✈ ✈ ✈
✈ ✈ ✈ ✈ ✈

MISSION #21 Saturday, April 22, 1944
HAMM

We went down to briefing at 1:00 p.m. and figured that we'd have a real nice, short mission over to the French coast and back, because it was so late. But briefing time doesn't mean a thing any more, because it stays light until 10:00 p.m.

Our target today was a very important industrial section and railroad yards at Hamm — very close to the Ruhr.

We took off at 4:00 p.m. and assembled at 20,000 feet. It was a rather short ride over, and there was very little flak and few fighters. Major Lee was leading our group. We reached the target about 7:00 p.m.; it was very clear, and we really plastered that place. The smoke was black and all over the sky. I could even see some of the buildings burning.

There were only a few bursts of flak in the area, but Major Lee's ship got one direct hit in a tank and went up in flames — but they all bailed out. The ship blew up shortly after.

We got back to the English coast about 9:00 p.m., and it was getting dark. By the time we got to the field, it was pitch black. I hadn't flown at night for more than six months, especially night formation, but it wasn't too bad. They had all the lights on, including a couple of searchlights.

The Germans followed us all the way home and shot down eight bombers while they milled around in the dark, trying to land. As soon as we got on the ground, they turned off everything. Sure gets dark around here.

✈ ✈ ✈ ✈ ✈
✈ ✈ ✈ ✈ ✈
✈ ✈ ✈ ✈ ✈
✈ ✈ ✈ ✈ ✈
✈

MISSION #22 Tuesday, April 25, 1944
METZ, FRANCE

We drew a milk run today. Drove into France and bombed an airfield where they train German pilots. We had a max load of fragmentation bombs — 2,800 lbs.

The mission was pretty easy — no fighters and very little flak. There were quite a few planes on the field, and I guess we blew them up.

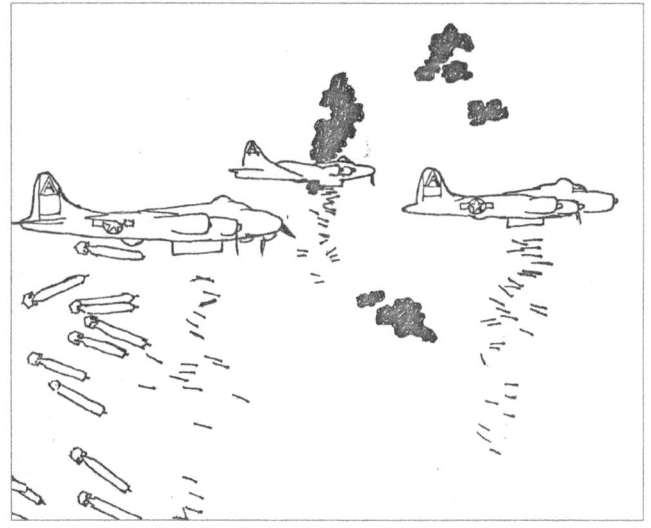

Our squadron CO, Col. Scheeler, led the wing today, and this was his last mission.

✈ ✈ ✈ ✈ ✈
✈ ✈ ✈ ✈ ✈
✈ ✈ ✈ ✈ ✈
✈ ✈ ✈ ✈ ✈
✈ ✈

MISSION #23 Thursday, April 27, 1944
CHERBOURG, FRANCE

Two in a row to France is very unusual for me. Seems like the only ones I draw are Berlin and the rest of the rough ones over the Reich.

Well, this was a pretty messy job. This Cherbourg is a flak house if I ever saw one. The target is just a few minutes into French territory. We took a 20-ship group over at 21,000 feet.

I led a flight up in the high squadron. We carried 6 thousand-pounders. We got over the target, but the lead bombardier couldn't pick it out because of the clouds. They sent up a barrage of flak so thick you could get out and walk on it — the worst flak I've seen since Berlin, and plenty accurate. They were bursting in between us all the time.

In about two minutes, they had hit about seven engines, and one boy took a direct hit and went down out of control. Nobody got out of the ship, and he hit the ground going straight down! Our ship had several holes in the wings, fuselage, and tail.

Nobody dropped their bombs on the target. The formation got hit so bad that it practically broke all up. I ended up leading the high squadron home.

✈ ✈ ✈ ✈ ✈
✈ ✈ ✈ ✈ ✈
✈ ✈ ✈ ✈ ✈
✈ ✈ ✈ ✈ ✈
✈ ✈ ✈

MISSION #24 Saturday, April 29, 1944
BERLIN (ABORTIVE)

We started out for the big city this morning. We took off at 7 o'clock in the morning, and we were carrying five 1000-lb. bombs. I was leading the second flight in the low squadron.

Had a hard time getting Lassie off the ground this morning. Sometimes you really sweat out a takeoff, especially if you're using the short runway, because each day, the bomb load is different. When the end of the runway comes up and you still don't have enough speed to get off, that's when the sweat starts rolling off of the forehead.

Lassie wasn't running so good today. She had a couple of bad engines, #1 and #2. We got up to altitude and got in formation anyway. #1 engine was running rough, and #2 was beginning to act up. We started across the Channel at 20,000 feet. By the time we got halfway across Belgium, the engines started to get worse, so I had to feather #1 and was afraid I'd have to do the same to #2. So I turned back, because it's useless to try to go in on three engines. You couldn't keep up with the formation, and, besides, you'd run out of gas.

The flak at the coast was pretty heavy, but we stayed above it and came back without getting hit. We got credit for a sortie, anyway.

✈ ✈ ✈ ✈ ✈
✈ ✈ ✈ ✈ ✈
✈ ✈ ✈ ✈ ✈
✈ ✈ ✈ ✈ ✈
✈ ✈ ✈ ✈

REST AND REHABILITATION May 5 to 14, 1944

One of the major problems for Air Force personnel while flying missions is combat fatigue. Many pilots and crew members alike, after several missions, become nervous wrecks. Some actually have nervous breakdowns. The flight surgeon is a very busy guy. His office is always crowded with men with these kinds of problems.

Up to this point, I have flown 24 missions, with not very much rest in between. We have had some very rough ones and a lot of pressure and stress: to Berlin three times in four or five days — and they were long, pressure-packed missions; on the mission to Schweinfurt, we were lucky to get back at all. That one took its toll on me. Physically and mentally, I am very tired and worn out, unable to get any sleep — especially on the night before a mission, and that's when you really need it. And on my last mission to Berlin, we came home on three engines, which was a big hassle and a pressure job.

In the interrogation room after our last Berlin mission, I was talking to Col. Scheeler, my group commander, a really swell guy. I was telling him about our problem, and I said, "I hope I don't have any more like today, because I don't think that I can handle it."

"It sounds like you've got combat fatigue." He knew about all of our tough missions. In fact, he went to bat for me on that Schweinfurt mission. He tried to get us credit for a mission, but couldn't. "Hey," he said, "you come into my office tomorrow morning."

"What for? Are you going to send me home? I hope!"

"No, but come in anyway."

So, the next morning, I went in. He handed me a memorandum. "Is this my discharge?" I asked.

He said, "No — read it." It said that I was supposed to pack enough clothes and personal belongings to last about 10 days, go to the train depot, and buy a ticket to some town in the southern part of England. "What for?" I asked. "What is this?"

"It's a rest-and-rehabilitation center for Air Force pilots." (I didn't even know that they had such places.) "I think you need a rest," he said.

In a couple of days, I had my stuff ready. I went to town, bought a ticket, and went. He had made arrangements, of course, and they had a room reserved for me. The train ride was about 3½ hours long. When I arrived at the town, a shuttle bus took us to the Center. I did not realize it at the time, but there were a few other guys on the train going to the same place.

When we got off the train, the weather was sunny and warm. We seldom ever see the sun back at the base; it's always either raining or foggy. This was much like Florida weather.

As we drove along this country road, we finally came to this huge, white, two-story English colonial house set in the center of a couple of acres of nicely cut green lawn, with many large trees and shrubs just beautifully landscaped. It looked like one of those old southern mansions. The house had about 30 rooms and was right on the bank of the Thames River. The banks of the Thames River also had nice green grass, right down to the water on both sides. You would always see people sitting on the grass by the water, and the water was clean. Not like in America, where most of the rivers are polluted and rubbish-strewn all along the banks.

There were about 25 guys here at this time, and most of them were fighter pilots from different places. I didn't know anyone, but it didn't take long to get acquainted. The place was run by the American Red Cross, but I imagine that Uncle Sam was picking up the tab.

All of the sleeping rooms were on the second floor, with a single bed and private bath. Downstairs there was a huge dining room, where everyone sat down together and had meals. There was a large recreation room with pool and ping-pong tables. There were writing tables and a reading room with hundreds of books. It was so peaceful and quiet — no airplanes roaring all day long, or army trucks, or sirens. It was similar to a retreat house. There was excellent home-cooked food and plenty of it, prepared by several women who were employed there.

Out in the river was a boat dock and several rowboats. There was also an area roped off in the water where we could swim. We were free to take a boat at any time and row up and down the river. The Thames River is not very wide, at least not at this particular spot; it's very calm, more like a channel, which made it more desirable for rowing a small boat.

I just loved it there. It was so remote that we hardly knew there was a war going on. Nobody ever talked about flying missions. We were all too busy having fun. There was a little town close by, and we were allowed to go there if we wanted to. It was a very small town; there was nothing much there except some stores and shops. The streets are all cobblestone. It was kind of interesting to walk around and look in shop windows.

There was one pub in the town, and it was in the lobby of their only hotel. That was the only place that you could buy a beer. There were not enough stools in the pub, so everyone would go in, buy a beer, and go out and sit in the lobby.

We got acquainted with a lot of nice people. The English people I met throughout my entire stay in England impressed me as being very courageous people. They never spoke of the war. They would talk about the weather, religion, politics — anything but war. During the first years of the war, they took a terrible beating from Germany and were on the brink of collapse, but they hung in there. They are good people, but their beer is lousy! They have Mild and Bitter; it looks dark, like molasses, and they serve it at room temperature.

I really enjoyed this place. More importantly, I got a good rest. Most of my time I spent in a boat on the river, or swimming, or just lying in the sun. I also read a lot. Although I hadn't done anything strenuous, my appetite had returned, and I was eating like there was no tomorrow. I was feeling good and getting a lot of sleep. I stayed for ten days; I gained my strength back — and also a few pounds.

Originally, the combat tour of duty was 25 missions. Shortly after we began, they increased it to 30. Now I was getting anxious to return to the base to fly those last six missions and get it over with, although I was dreading the very thought of it.

MISSION #25 Thursday, May 18, 1944
BERLIN

Well, if it weren't for the great Doolittle, I'd be through with combat now. But the boy says we have to go five more, so I guess we'll have to do it. I sure wish he'd get off of his dead seat and fly a couple of missions. Then he'd probably change his mind.

We put up two groups from here today. I led a flight way up in the high squadron of the high group. I was at 26,000 feet.

We went in the long way — over the North Sea, to Norway, and then down to Germany. We had some major leading the wing today who didn't know his rear from a two-dollar bill. He never held a good airspeed at any time and practically stalled the whole formation out at times.

It was a long ride into the target. We hit it about 2 o'clock. The flak was very thick over the city, as usual.

I saw a pack of German fighters hit a group of Forts on the right of us. There must have been at least 50 of them, and they came in all at once, head on. They knocked out a couple of bombers.

We didn't get any fighter attacks — thank God! It sure makes you sweat when you see them hit some outfit close by. You just sit there and wait and wonder when they are going to hit you. We dropped our load of incendiaries over the middle of the city and started for home.

The ride home is always the longest drive. It seemed like it took a year to get from Norway to England. I hate to fly over that darn sea! Because when we come home, we are invariably sweating out the gas and the engines. Usually we have just enough gas to get to the field. The only time England looks good is when you're coming back from Germany!

We logged 9 hours and 50 minutes on this drive. Was a pretty good show — and the fifth trip over the capital for me. I hope it's the last!

✈ ✈ ✈ ✈ ✈
✈ ✈ ✈ ✈ ✈
✈ ✈ ✈ ✈ ✈
✈ ✈ ✈ ✈ ✈
✈ ✈ ✈ ✈ ✈

MISSION #26 Monday, May 22, 1944
KIEL

We bombed some shipyards at Kiel today. We carried a maximum load of incendiaries. Our route in was over the sea. The mission was 7 hours long, and about 5 hours were over the North Sea.

The flak was pretty good over the target. We saw a few Forts get hit. One boy blew up right in front of us. There were a few Jerries around, but the P-38s gave them plenty of trouble.

✈ ✈ ✈ ✈ ✈
✈ ✈ ✈ ✈ ✈
✈ ✈ ✈ ✈ ✈
✈ ✈ ✈ ✈ ✈
✈ ✈ ✈ ✈ ✈
✈

MISSION #27 Tuesday, May 23, 1944
SAARBRÜCKEN, GERMANY

I led the low squadron today in the new 12-ship group. We bombed something at Saarbrücken. The weather was solid over the target. We dropped on pathfinders. The mission was 7 hours long.

The flak was pretty heavy at the coast going in. A group on our left was hit hard. One Fort blew up instantly, and another went down covered with flames and exploded before it hit the ground. However, I think the whole crew bailed out.

We missed all the flak going in. There was some moderate flak over the target. A few bursts came pretty close, just enough to make us sweat a little. I saw a few dogfights. Our escort was excellent, and the fighters didn't get close to us. We came out without any flak at the Belgium coast.

✈ ✈ ✈ ✈ ✈
✈ ✈ ✈ ✈ ✈
✈ ✈ ✈ ✈ ✈
✈ ✈ ✈ ✈ ✈
✈ ✈ ✈ ✈ ✈
✈ ✈

MISSION #28 Wednesday, May 24, 1944
NANCY, FRANCE

The weather was perfectly clear today over France, so we took advantage of it. We hit airfields at Nancy, deep into France. I led the low squadron again, and we flew the 12-ship group. I always hate to lead that low squadron, because it's the hardest of the two.

We went over at 20,000 feet. The flak at the coast was light, and nobody got hit. There were at least 800 heavy bombers over France today, and almost every wing was bombing different airfields.

We hit our target on the nose. I saw six different targets that were hit, and the smoke was as high as we were over some of them. It was some of the best bombing that I've ever seen.

We didn't have any fighter attacks, but there were packs of Jerries in the area, and our fighters were having a field day.

✈ ✈ ✈ ✈ ✈
✈ ✈ ✈ ✈ ✈
✈ ✈ ✈ ✈ ✈
✈ ✈ ✈ ✈ ✈
✈ ✈ ✈ ✈ ✈
✈ ✈ ✈

MISSION #29 Saturday, May 27, 1944
DESSAU, GERMANY

This is one section of the Reich that I don't care if I ever see again. Dessau is south of Berlin and close to Leipzig, where there are always lots of German fighters. We were supposed to bomb an assembly shop and airfield at Dessau. I was Deputy Group Leader today. We went in at 23,000 feet. Our bomb load was ten 500-pounders.

We sure took a cook's tour of Germany today. Our route took us in way north of the target and then down and around and out through the southern part of Germany.

The wing leader, whoever he was, sure had his head up and locked, because he flew over every flak battery in the country. The target area was about 60% covered with clouds. The flak over the target was very heavy, and it was close. I sure sweated the darn stuff out too, because I didn't want to get hit on my 29th raid.

Our group dropped our bombs on the first run over the target and were darn glad to get out of the flak. In the meantime, the leader group and high groups didn't drop theirs and were going to make another bomb run, so, naturally, we had to stay in formation for protection against fighter attacks. They finally made a 360-degree turn, and we all drove through the flak once again. That is exactly how the Eighth Air Force loses about 30% of their ships, just making 360-degree turns over the target. They lost a couple of ships out of the lead and high groups. One blew up right in formation.

The ride home was very long and tiresome. There were flocks of German fighters around the target. They knocked the hell out of a group behind us. They made a pass at one outfit, and three Forts went down. One blew up, another was going down with a couple of engines smoking, and the third was in a terrific spin.

We had a little flak coming out of the enemy coast, but it wasn't very accurate. That English Channel sure looked good to me, because I knew that I'd have to sweat out that coast just one more time. That flak really works on a guy's mind. Every time you go over, it keeps running through your mind, I wonder if they will get me today. And the longer you go, the worse you get.

However, I think I can take one more. But not any more than one, because I'm plenty tired of sweating these raids out, and besides, I'm getting awfully tired physically. In fact, I feel like an old man at 25. Here's hoping for an easy one to finish on!!

✈ ✈ ✈ ✈ ✈
✈ ✈ ✈ ✈ ✈
✈ ✈ ✈ ✈ ✈
✈ ✈ ✈ ✈ ✈
✈ ✈ ✈ ✈ ✈
✈ ✈ ✈ ✈

MISSION #30 Monday, May 29, 1944
DESSAU, GERMANY

Easy one, heck!

I had a funny feeling this morning when the alert officer woke me up at 2:30 a.m. I just figured it was going to be a tough one. I could hear that guy come up the stairs. I don't think I slept more than an hour last night.

We went back to Dessau again today. I don't know how I ever drew this one to finish up on. I flew Deputy Group Leader again today, and we were in the low group.

Everything seemed wrong ever since we got up this morning. The weather at the base was bad. The fog was so thick you couldn't see the end of the runway. Instead of taking off in 30-second intervals, we had to take off at one-minute intervals to let the ship ahead of us get up through the soup, because he'd disappear about three-fourths of the way down the runway. The assembly was bad also, because of the clouds and dense contrails. However, we finally got the formation together, but the wing formation consisted of only two groups. One group couldn't get off the ground because of the fog. I knew that if we went in with only two groups, we'd be a cinch to be jumped by fighters. And sure enough, we did.

Our wing leader, Col. Milton, played it pretty cozy. He tried to stay as close to other formations as much as possible, and, in doing so, we had to go up to 25,000 feet and pick up a lot of speed to catch these other outfits, who were about 8 minutes ahead of us.

I had Lassie wide open all day long. I knew darn well if I used full power for 8 hours with a load, I'd either burn up an engine or run out of gas. But I didn't have an alternative. It was either stay in formation or get picked off like a pigeon. I figured that, this being my last mission, I'd do everything possible to keep the big bird flying!

It was a long, rough ride to the target. We finally got there, and the wings turned off to their respective targets, which left our two little groups sticking out like a sore thumb. And, of all times, our target was further west and closer to Berlin than the rest. When we got to the IP, the flak started coming up; it was the best flak I've ever seen, and it was plenty thick. In fact, it was so thick that we could barely see the group ahead of us. Our bomb run was unusually long, and we drove through all that flak with our bomb-bay doors open. Every time I'd hear a burst of flak, I'd think we'd been hit in the bomb bay with the load still there.

The bomb run is the tensest moment of a mission, always expecting a burst of flak to explode the bombs. We finally got the bombs away, which was a big relief. But as soon as we got out of the flak, I spotted a bunch of fighters off to our right who were racing toward us. I can always tell the Germans by the way they fly, in bunches. No formation whatsoever, and they always seem to be going about 400 mph. There must have been fifty of them in this bunch, and they were coming around to the front of us to make their attack. They were twin-engine fighters.

We pulled our formation in closer together, and, just as they peeled off for the kill, our leader turned away from them, which made them overshoot us a little. That was a very smart move, because if they would have had a good run on us, they would have cleaned house on our little 35-ship formation. They came in anyway, and everyone did a little individual evasive action. But unfortunately, I zigged when I should have zagged, and one of them hit my #1 engine. It smoked a little bit, and I thought they had me, but I hit the feathering switch and had it stopped in no time flat.

Now I had a devil of a time trying to stay in formation with three engines, so I had to drop out. We had three more hours to go before we got to the Channel, and then I really began to worry, because if the Germans came back and caught me out of formation, it would be curtains! The only thing I could do was to lose altitude and stay below the formation and as close as possible. I did that for a while, and I gradually kept dropping back until I was all alone.

We were pretty lucky that the fighters didn't come back. About 30 minutes later, a couple of P-51s flew up alongside of us and escorted us all the way back to England, for which I was very grateful. I guess the reason the Germans didn't show up again was that a group of P-47s were on them like a suntan right after they made a pass at us.

We got back to the Channel OK. Got shot at a couple of times by a few flak batteries, but we dodged them. I was never so glad to see England in my life.

✈ ✈ ✈ ✈ ✈
✈ ✈ ✈ ✈ ✈
✈ ✈ ✈ ✈ ✈
✈ ✈ ✈ ✈ ✈
✈ ✈ ✈ ✈ ✈
✈ ✈ ✈ ✈ ✈

Record of Missions

1. Saturday, January 29, 1944 Frankfurt
2. Sunday, January 30, 1944 Brunswick
   – 3 days off –
3. Thursday, February 3, 1944 Wilhelmshaven
4. Friday, February 4, 1944 Frankfurt
5. Saturday, February 5, 1944 Burgess, France
   – 14 days off –
6. Monday, February 20, 1944 Oschersleben
7. Tuesday, February 21, 1944 Osnabrück
8. Friday, February 24, 1944 Schweinfurt
9. Saturday, February 25, 1944 Augsburg
   – 8 days off –
10. Monday, March 6, 1944 Berlin

– 1 day off –

11. Wednesday, March 8, 1944 Berlin

12. Thursday, March 9, 1944 Berlin
    – 8 days off –

13. Saturday, March 18, 1944 Oberpfaffenhofen
    – 1 day off –

14. Monday, March 20, 1944 Frankfurt
    – 1 day off –

15. Wednesday, March 22, 1944 Berlin

16. Thursday, March 23, 1944 Munster
    Friday, March 24, 1944 Schweinfurt – ABORTIVE
    – 3 days off –

17. Tuesday, March 28, 1944 Reims, France

18. Wednesday, March 29, 1944 Brunswick
    – 9 days off –

19. Saturday, April 8, 1944 Oldenburg
    – 4 days off –

20. Thursday, April 13, 1944 Schweinfurt
    – 8 days off –

21. Saturday, April 22, 1944 Hamm
    – 2 days off –

22. Tuesday, April 25, 1944 Metz, France
– 1 day off –

23. Thursday, April 27, 1944 Cherbourg, France
– 1 day off –

24. Saturday, April 29, 1944 Berlin – ABORTIVE
– 18 days off –

* Friday, May 5 through Sunday, May 14, 1944 Rest and Rehabilitation

25. Thursday, May 18, 1944 Berlin
– 3 days off –

26. Monday, May 22, 1944 Kiel

27. Tuesday, May 23, 1944 Saarbrücken

28. Wednesday, May 24, 1944 Nancy, France
– 2 days off –

29. Saturday, May 27, 1944 Dessau, Germany
– 1 day off –

30. Monday, May 29, 1944 Dessau, Germany

Eight days later:

Tuesday, June 6, 1944 — D-Day — Invasion of Normandy

180 ✈ WINGS IN THE HANDS OF THE LORD

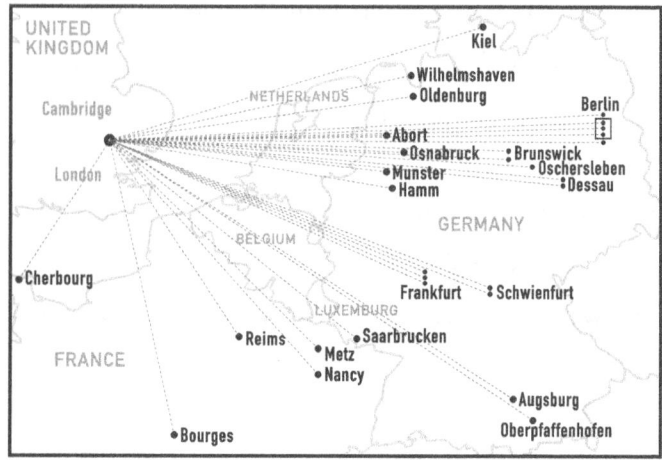

Page 6   MINNEAPOLIS DAILY TIMES   Sat., July 1, 1944

Flies 30 Missions, None of Crew Hurt

Five times over Berlin and 25 times over other sections of Germany, First Lieut. Louis La Hood, 3058 Hayes St. N.E., has brought back "Lassie Come Home," his Flying Fortress, every time without a wounded or injured crew member. He wears the DFC. He describes his first trip as typical of the rest. Ugly black patches of flak, he said, made the sky look stormy. A few unfortunates were going down; others were feathering props to straggle back into formation. The plane on his left blew up. He closed in, filling that position. The enemy fighters swept through again. Then Allied fighters appeared, "a beautiful sight," and nursed them home.

Lieut. La Hood

Peoria Pilot Is Awarded Many Medals For Combat

Decorated with the Distinguished Flying Cross and the Air Medal with three Oak Leaf clusters, and wearing a bronze Battle Star on his theater ribbon, designating combat with the enemy, 24-year-old First Lt. Louis LaHood of Peoria is one of the outstanding Flying Fortress pilots with an Eighth AAF Bomber unit stationed in England.

Five times over Berlin and 25 times over other sections of Germany and enemy-occupied countries is the score set thus far by Lieutenant LaHood, according to a story received by the Journal-Transcript today from the public relations office of headquarters, United States strategic air forces, in Europe.

LaHood is the son of John LaHood, St. Francis hospital, and the brother of Mrs. Michael Unes and Mrs. Alice LaHood of 515 Smith st. His brother, George, is in an Army anti-aircraft division in California.

LT. LOUIS LA HOOD

CHAPTER 17

Homeward Bound

Our last few missions were the longest. I finished my tour of duty on the last day of May. The invasion of France, D-Day — the Normandy Invasion, took place on June 6, 1944, six days after I had flown my 30th mission. Because I had flown my first two missions before the rest of my crew began theirs, they had two more missions to fly after mine were complete and before we could leave England for home. Joe, my co-pilot, flew those last two missions as first pilot, and he had a fill-in co-pilot. The crew finished up their tour that way. Now that all of us had completed our work, we were sent to a debarkation center up in Manchester, England, where we were to board a transport ship and return home to America.

I was glad they didn't ask me to fly a plane back to the States. I was tired and just wanted to relax now and ride a boat back home. After waiting for a ship in Manchester for nearly three weeks, we finally embarked on our journey homeward to America. It was sometime in June 1944. The weather was pleasant and warm. The trip was very relaxing, as we lay on the deck all day, soaking up the sun, and getting tanned. Our crossing took 13 days. We probably didn't take a straight course, because during wartime, troop ships had to be ever alert for submarines and, for that matter, any kind of enemy attack. I think our ship did a lot of zigzagging. Food on the ship was plentiful and super-good — lots of steaks and just everything good.

We docked in New York Harbor and stayed on the ship overnight. Imagine having several hundreds of homesick guys penned up on a troop ship all night in the harbor. We were like animals trying to get out of a cage. When we were ready to get off the next day, all of us had envisioned the civilians of New York welcoming us back home, as we had so often seen such things in the movies — you know, a band out to meet the veterans, people cheering, etc., etc. Well, let me tell you, it was nothing like that. Nobody even looked up at us as we marched off the boat. Everybody was in a hurry to get to work or wherever they were rushing to. If you got in their way on the sidewalk, they would just shove you aside. New York, and the people in it, was the coldest, most unfriendly city. I said then that I would never go back to that place as long as I live. I never have.

From the ship, we were marched directly to the train depot, where we boarded a troop train, still not knowing where we were going. Truthfully, most of us didn't care, as long as we got out of New York City. During the war, the Air Force had taken over some of the swanky hotels at Miami Beach, Florida, and used them for rehabilitation centers for returning combat personnel. It was unbelievable. We were taken straight to Miami Beach and put up in those swanky hotels. I was in the Fontainebleau Hotel. Although I never did understand the purpose for it, we went through many interrogation sessions, answered hundreds of questions, and were analyzed by many psychiatrists. I suppose they wanted to know what effect combat missions had on persons who had been through them. We were given all kinds of physical and mental tests. Many of the tests were crazy. For example, the psychiatrists would give us a jumbled-up picture that made no sense at all and then ask us to give our own version of what the picture meant. I couldn't have cared less at that time; I would just give them anything that came to my mind. They must have thought that I was nuts or shell-shocked or something, because they kept me there for about three weeks. In the meantime, I was enjoying the beach and the golf course and the nightclubs.

Eventually, they asked me if I would like to go to a rest home in St. Petersburg, Florida, or back to duty. I didn't like the sound of that "back-to-duty" bit, so I said, of course, "I would like to go to St. Petersburg." Returning B-17 pilots were being sent to the islands in the South Pacific to fly B-29s, and I was afraid I might be among them. I didn't want any part of the South Pacific or of B-29s. So they sent me and several others of us to St. Pete.

At St. Pete, we were right on the beach in a very large building that may have been a hotel at one time but had been converted into a rest home for returning Air Force men. It was beautiful, and so was the location. Maids took care of our rooms, and the food was great. Although we were required to attend a couple of lectures every day and to participate in all of the rehabilitating functions such as swimming, softball, tennis, movies, and golf, being there was marvelous. The doctors and psychiatrists there were constantly checking us, but every time they asked us if we were still pretty nervous, we, of course, said "Yes." We didn't want to leave that place. In fact, whenever a doctor was present, we acquired a twitch of some kind so that he would mark on your chart "Needs more rehabilitation." Really, there wasn't a thing wrong with any of us, but I figured that if this was for the Air Force vets, why not take advantage of it? I stayed there for two months. David George, my cousin from Minneapolis, was stationed across the bay at Tampa at that time. He came to visit me, and we had a good time. We swam in the ocean and went into town. He stayed for a weekend, I think.

Lou and cousin David George
Tampa, Florida
Summer 1944

After two months of that pleasant life, I actually began feeling guilty, so I asked to be shipped out, thinking that would perhaps speed up my discharge. Instead, I was ordered to report to none other than Lockbourne Air Base to be an instructor in B-17s. Lockbourne is where I had taken my training, so I was not too disappointed.

CHAPTER 18

Closing the Circle

When I arrived back at Lockbourne, I had to be checked out again because I hadn't flown for more than three months.

I took a little refresher course, after which I was supposed to start instructing. By then, there were beginning to be more returning pilots who were also expecting to instruct, but there were not many students. They were rotating the instructors at Lockbourne who had not been to combat. As I was walking to my quarters one day, someone yelled at me. I turned around, and there, to my amazement, was Bill Martin, my cocky little instructor from basic training. "What are you doing here?" I asked.

"I'm a student in training for combat," he told me.

I could hardly keep from laughing in his face, though I wanted to really lay it on him. This is the guy I had lain awake nights dreaming of ways to murder. He was full of questions: about combat, about how many missions I had done, about whether it was hard, and about how often we got shot up. *This is one way I can get back at him,* I figured, so I laid it on thick and heavy.

"It was so rough that I just spent two months in a rest hospital," I told him. His face was showing some concern. Going on, I said, "I hear you guys are going over to the islands to fight the Japs." He turned pale and left without saying much more. *Wouldn't it be funny now,* I thought, *if I got him for a student!* But I didn't, and, for that matter, I didn't ever see him again.

Actually, I didn't do much of anything at Lockbourne. I instructed for only about a month. My cousin Virgil George was stationed there and working as an aircraft mechanic. One weekend, three of us pilots got permission to take a trip to Florida. I asked Virgil if he wanted to go and, in fact, requested that he come and be our crew chief. He came, and we went to Miami. After landing at Boca Raton Air Base, we drove to Miami, where Virgil and I looked up some Lebanese friends who took us in, put on a very nice meal for us, and provided us a very pleasant evening. It was an enjoyable trip. The next day, we returned to Ohio.

It was now December 1944. We were doing nothing but sitting around. I couldn't figure out why they didn't discharge me. I was anxiously awaiting the time when I could get out. About that time, I received orders to report to Roswell, New Mexico. Why I had to go there, I couldn't figure out. When I asked the officer in charge if I could refuse the assignment, he said, "No, you'd better not. It might delay your discharge."

I might as well go, I thought. With 15 days before I was due to report, I decided I might as well go to Peoria first. So

*Lou with cousin and fellow Peorian, Virgil George
Lockbourne Air Base, Columbus, Ohio
December 1944*

downtown I went, bought a used car — a 1938 Buick, black, two-door — paid for it, drove to a gas station, filled it with gas and oil, and started for Peoria, arriving there in time to spend Christmas of 1944 and New Year's Eve at home. Even though a lot of the guys were still in the service, I had a very nice time in Peoria during the holidays.

On New Year's day, driving my newly acquired used car, I set out for Roswell, New Mexico. Cars, believe it or not, were scarce and hard to get at that time. Automobile manufacturers had not made any cars for three or four years during the war, because all of their plants had been transformed for the manufacture of tanks, trucks, and all kinds of war vehicles. So cars were hard to get, and practically everyone was satisfied to drive any kind of used car that they could get.

All alone, I found the trip to New Mexico very boring. Making the trip took me about three days, but amazingly, I made it without a bit of trouble — not even a flat tire. Upon my arrival there, I reported to the office of the commanding officer and asked what my specific duties were going to be. I was told to go back to my quarters and to stand by for an assignment. I stood by for a week, two weeks, three weeks — with no word as to what I was supposed to do. So, I did nothing.

I was not alone, though. Many combat pilots like me, who had returned from overseas, were also sitting around, standing by, waiting for word. In the meantime, we were being fed and paid, so we didn't much mind. I had my car, and I was free to come and go when I pleased. No one ever checked up on us. We went to town every night, and, on the weekends, we rode around to several little towns just to see the sights. In order to receive our flying pay, $150 a month, in addition to our regular wages — which for a first lieutenant at that time were $525 per month — we were required to fly only four hours a month. Except for the few hours of flying, I did not do one solitary thing at that place.

After the fourth week, I was transferred to Williams Field in Phoenix, Arizona. Again, I drove. Phoenix was a lot nicer — the weather was beautiful, and there was a lot to do in the town. It was almost the beginning of March 1945.

At Phoenix, just as at Roswell, we had nothing to do, either, so, I played a lot of golf. Why they just didn't discharge us, I couldn't understand. I flew a lot more at Phoenix, because it was enjoyable. When you are not flying in combat, it is so easy and relaxing. Flying around for the fun of it is a snap. We ferried a lot of planes from Phoenix to Colorado and other air bases.

Although I don't recall the exact details, the Air Force was beginning to work out a point system for the purpose of releasing people from service. It involved a certain number of points for your length of service, a certain number for time spent overseas, a certain number for how much combat you had taken part in, and so forth. Finally, when the point system had been all worked out and the Air Force determined how many points each man had according to his service record, I was informed that I had enough points to be discharged. I was notified about the first part of May 1945.

Before I accepted the discharge, however, I was given the option of remaining for another four years, with an immediate promotion to captain and assignment to another group — probably to do another tour of combat. I wanted no part of that. They also gave me another alternative — of remaining in the Inactive Reserves and being subject to call at any time in case of another national emergency. I didn't want any part of that, either. I wanted a discharge — to be completely detached from military service. I had had enough.

Later on in life, I often wondered if I had made the right decision. Had I stayed in the Air Force and made a career of it, I could have retired with 20 years and a pretty good pension, at the age of 40 or 42. But who knows? You can't look back and say, "I should have done this or that." Anyway, at that point in my life, I was tired of military regulations and traveling from one base to another. I wanted to go home.

I was released from Williams Field, Arizona, and was to report to Fort Sheridan, Illinois, for discharge. Since I still had my car, I drove home. A friend, who was also to report to Fort Sheridan, rode with me. We took our time, stopping along the way, as we were not required to be there by a specified time. This was the most relaxing trip. We knew we were going home. We knew there would be no more assignments and no more pressure. We had a lot of fun along the way.

At Fort Sheridan, a lot of paperwork and processing awaited us. In fact, it took about as long to be discharged as it had to be inducted into the service. Finally, on May 24, 1945, I was released from Fort Sheridan. I was free to go home! I did not go directly home, however. As long as I was so close to Chicago, I decided to go there, spend the weekend, and visit some friends. Again, I enjoyed myself, and, after a couple of days, I headed for Peoria.

CHAPTER 19

A Civilian Once Again

Returning to Peoria in 1945 was kind of strange, because all of my friends were still in the service. I was one of the first to be discharged on the point system. Peoria was booming; the saloons were doing a land-office business. The town was full of servicemen from an Army base nearby. I was having a good time spending my $300 mustering-out pay. For about two months, I did not work, not because I did not want to, but mostly because there were not a lot of jobs to be had. And I was not particularly anxious to start working at just any old job.

I had applied for a flying job with TWA and American Airlines, and I was waiting around, hoping for an answer from them. In the meantime, I took a job in a factory for a couple of months. But I didn't like it at all, and so I quit. I missed flying, so occasionally, I would go out to the Peoria

Airport, rent a plane, and fly a little. Of course, I had to get checked out again by an instructor.

When I was at the airport one day, I had to present my flying license before taking a plane. The airport manager noticed that I had a multi-engine rating and an instrument rating. He asked me what I had flown. I told him that I had flown single-engine, twin-engine, and four-engine planes, and that I had just gotten out of the Air Force. He asked me if I would like to come to work for him as his charter pilot. He told me that he was going to buy a surplus twin-engine plane from the government and asked if I would go with him to North Carolina and fly it back. Even though I hadn't flown a twin-engine since training two years before, I assured him that I could manage it. A couple of days later, we left by train for North Carolina.

At the airport in North Carolina, hundreds of Air Force training planes were gathered, waiting to be either sold or junked. He bought one — a twin-engine Cessna Bobcat, just like the one I had flown in advanced training. Flying it was a snap, and even though I had been used to flying a big four-engine bomber, it took me only a few minutes to adjust to this smaller craft. I took it up and shot some takeoffs and landings for a while, and then I was ready to fly it back home. We took off and flew back to Peoria, where he then began having the plane remodeled for use as a charter plane, capable of carrying five people.

We put it in the hangar, and he put all of his mechanics to work on it. In a few weeks, it was like new, painted red and white, and the seats freshly re-upholstered in red leather. The plane looked beautiful, and I was the pilot. I was kept pretty busy flying customers to Chicago, St. Louis, Indianapolis, and other cities. Then, too, I flew the owner to many airplane factories. As a result, I was gone a lot and didn't have much free time for anything else. I flew that plane for about a year, after which time I began to find the routine monotonous, and, in addition, I thought I was being underpaid.

Besides, the job was hazardous. I had to fly into a lot of small fields and in all kinds of weather. Some of those small air fields were not equipped with radio towers or proper lighting. To add to everything else, the maintenance crew he had did not satisfy me. In the Air Force, I was used to having excellent maintenance crews, whose mechanics really knew how to care for engines, because they had been properly trained by the Air Force. But I didn't have the same level of confidence in my new employer's maintenance crew. I didn't know if they were keeping the engines in top running condition. I didn't know if they ever changed the oil when it was supposed to be changed or checked for loose oil lines or leaks in gas or brake lines. Sometimes when I had an early-morning trip scheduled, I would get the plane out and find it hadn't even been gassed up. Little things like that happened all the time, and I was getting disgusted.

In the meantime, I had received an answer from TWA and American Airlines thanking me for my application and explaining that their policy at that time was not to hire returning military pilots, preferring instead, to train their own. If, in the future, they had a change of policy, they said, they would contact me.

If I couldn't fly for a big company, I decided that I might as well get out of aviation completely and find something else. I quit my job flying the charter plane, and that ended my flying career. It was a lot of fun for the four years it lasted.

I had many thrills and, of course, many tense moments, too. I loved it all — all that I experienced in the Air Force.

After I quit the charter plane, Gene Bettenhaus, another pilot, was hired to take my place. He flew it for about four months. One night when he was returning from a trip, he got lost, ran out of gas, crashed, and was killed. I have always thought since, *Who knows? That might have happened to me.*

Epilogue

Lou LaHood was honorably discharged from the Eighth Air Force in May 1945 with the rank of 1st Lieutenant. He had been assigned to the 91st Bomb Group, 322nd Bomb Squadron. He earned the following awards:

- The Distinguished Flying Cross
- The Air Medal with Three Bronze Oak Leaf Clusters
- The Presidential Unit Citation
- The American Campaign Medal
- The European-African-Middle Eastern Campaign Medal with Two Bronze Service Stars
- The World War II Victory Medal
- An Honorable Service Lapel Button

In August 1946, he married Margaret Kouri in Peoria, Illinois. They had four children: Diane, Jim, Mary, and Peggy. He owned and operated a famous Peoria restaurant, Lou's Drive In, for 40 years. After his death in 1993 from an aggressive brain tumor, the family continued to operate it until 2014, and, at this writing, it is still thriving under the same name.

In addition to military awards, Lou earned recognition in his ancestral homeland. His parents had emigrated from the tiny village of Aytou, Lebanon, at the turn of the twentieth century. When a cousin from Aytou visited the large contingent of descendants living in Peoria in the late 1980s, Lou and his family were surprised and pleased to learn that he was famous there, being known as The Lebanese Eagle.

Shadow Box
Military Honors

Army Air Forces 1945

Margaret and Lou
August 1946

Lou at his newly opened restaurant, July 1953

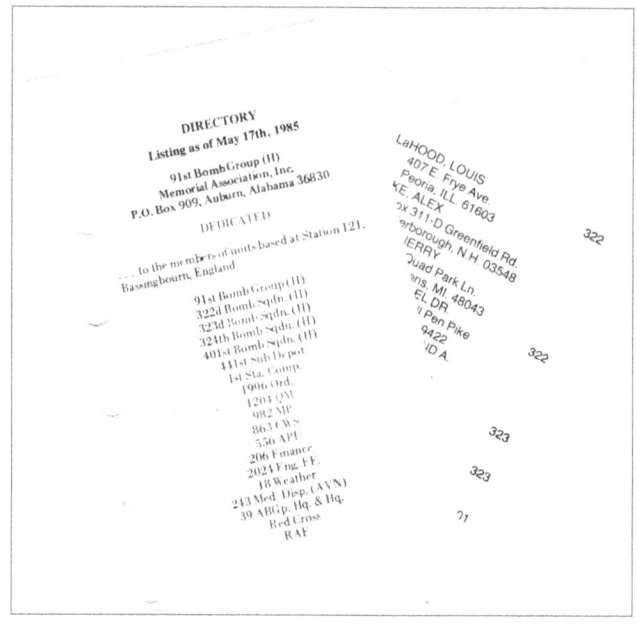

1985 List of Veterans in the 91st Bomb Group

*Lou and son Jim
Peoria airport, B-17 Fly-In
Circa 1990*

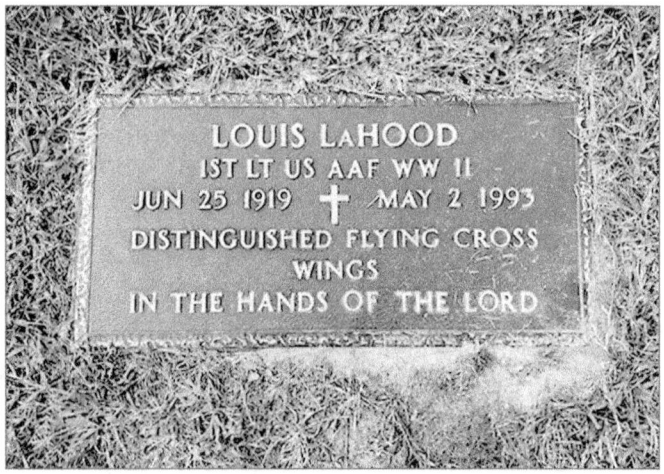

Placed at the foot of Lou's and Margaret's gravesite

About the Authors

Louis LaHood was born in Minneapolis, MN in 1919. He came to Peoria, IL as a teenager to live with an elder sister and her family. After the war, he returned to Peoria, married and raised a family, and was a successful businessman until his death in 1993.

Jim LaHood is a retired design engineer, and the son of Louis and Margaret LaHood. In 1977, reading his father's newly-written memoir, Jim was struck by the quiet strength and faith in God that carried him through WWII, and the rest of his life.

www.ingramcontent.com/pod-product-compliance
Lightning Source LLC
Chambersburg PA
CBHW071431080526
44587CB00014B/1802